A Simple Recipe for Stealing the Wealth of a Nation

A-basic-guide to accumulating massive wealth at the expense of the American citizens

Thomas DeForge

Published by FastPencil

Copyright © 2013 Thomas DeForge

Published by FastPencil
3131 Bascom Ave.
Suite 150
Campbell CA 95008 USA
info@fastpencil.com
(408) 540-7571
(408) 540-7572 (Fax)
http://www.fastpencil.com

No part of this publication may be reproduced, stored in a retrieval system, or transmitted, in any form, or by any means, electronic, mechanical, photocopying, recording, or otherwise, without the prior consent of the publisher.

The Publisher makes no representations or warranties with respect to the accuracy or completeness of the contents of this book and specifically disclaim any implied warranties of merchantability or fitness for a particular purpose. Neither the publisher nor author shall be liable for any loss of profit or any commercial damages.

Printed in the United States of America.

First Edition

This book is dedicated to both my children and all the children of this nation. It is with a heavy heart that my generation and those that preceded it leave you this once great nation in a condition inconceivable to its founding principles. It is my fervent hope for your generation, that enough Americans awake from their slumber in order to change the course of our nation and save it from the tyranny that has taken root over the last one hundred years.

Acknowledgments

I would like to not thank, but rather acknowledge the many politicians both past and present along with the member banks and their owners that make up the Federal Reserve System that have conspired together to steal the wealth of the American people.

Without all of your dedication to your own self-serving purpose, this book simply would not be possible or necessary.

I would like to thank a dear friend whose superb mastery of the English language was crucial to this writting. For personal reasons she has asked to remain anonymous.

Contents

	Preface	ix
Chapter 1	Depressions, a Bit of History	1
Chapter 2	Ingredients for Creating the Greatest of Depressions	7
Chapter 3	Dumbing Down Your Nation	41
Chapter 4	Keep Your Nation Busy	51
Chapter 5	The End Game	79
Chapter 6	Saving a Nation	91
Chapter 7	The Idiocracy of Our Democracy	111
Chapter 8	By Accident or Design the End Knows no Difference	135
Chapter 9	What to Do	161
	Conclusion	171

Preface

Understanding and having the ability to create a national depression can deliver untold wealth beyond imagination. It will allow you to steal from literally millions of people their personal wealth on a scale that is inconceivable to most. If you follow this simple recipe, the road to creating these depressions is filled with opportunity and profits beyond the visions of the common man. The great thing about this is that anyone can do it without investing a dime of their own money.

It will require a few personal attributes however in order to ensure your success. You must have the ability to lie and deceive, be a thief at heart, exhibit no integrity, show little to no concern for your fellow man and have the uncanny ability to turn a blind eye to humankind altogether. If you possess these attributes, you may very well be a candidate for success and could possibly acquire wealth beyond your wildest dreams.

1

DEPRESSIONS, A BIT OF HISTORY

Creating a depression on a national scale takes careful planning and manipulation. While depressions are a normal phenomenon that take place from time to time in any economy, creating one on a national scale requires a level of intentional, well-crafted careful preparation and influence from an outside source. Without this influence, *depressions* tend to be more localized and rarely if ever occur on a national scale. In an economy uninfluenced and left to the natural laws of economics, depressions tend to be more segmented, impacting only areas of the economy that have become overextended or areas in which production surpasses demand.

What is common to all *national depressions* is that in order to create or suffer a depression on a national scale, the government must first *control that nation's money supply* or dictate what that money supply should be. Second, the government of that nation must in some form practice intervention into that nation's economy. Nations in which governments intervene or control their economy practice either the *socialist* or *communist* philosophy. Nations whose governments do not intervene in the economy but prefer to leave the economy to the consumption and production patterns of the nations citizens practice *capitalism* as their economic philosophy.

What few Americans know or understand, is that America's economic philosophy was altered from *capitalism* to *socialism* about one hundred years ago. The foundation was layed in 1913, and the full transformation occured in the 1930s. I know this is a bit of information that is hard to swallow and at first will seem absolutely ludicrous to the majority of the readers. However, if you read on, you too may find this statement to be true. The deception that the United States has been and still is a *capitalistic* society (like our forefathers intended) over the last century, has been nothing more than an illusion. One necessary and imperative to maintain as a handful of talented theives set into motion the ingredients in this recipe allowing them to steal the wealth of this once great nation.

Prior to America adopting the *socialist philosophy*, depressions did not occur on the level of the first Great Depression neither in duration or severity. While depressions/recessions are a natural occurrence in any society, in a *"free"* or pure capitalistic society, boom and bust cycles are relatively localized and impact smaller areas or pockets of a nation. The United States has suffered several depressions, one of the worst being the Great Depression which started in 1929 and lasted through the 1930s. The Great Depression is what I consider the first depression that the United States experienced under socialist ideals.

Let's take a closer look at the history of American depression/recession occurrences:

- 1797-lasted 3 years.
- 1807-lasted 6 years.
- 1819-lasted two years.
- 1832-lasted two years.
- 1836-lasted six years.
- 1857-lasted two years.
- 1869-lasted two years.
- 1873-lasted 5 years.
- 1896-lasted 3 years.
- 1901- lasted 1 year.
- 1907-Bank failures (intentionally created by the largest bankers).
- 1913-U.S. nationalized the banking system. (onset of the socialist philosophy).
- 1920-lasted 2 years.
- 1929-lasted 11 years (total transformation to socialism).

If we take a look at both the historical length and time span between these depressions, we can see that prior to socialism taking root in America, depressions lasted on average of two and a half years and occurred on average once every eleven and a quarter years. Once America began to socialize its economic philosophy (1913), it created a depression that lasted eleven years, or three hunderd forty percent longer than the average of previous depressions. The 1930s Great Depression, was the only depression in our history in which the nation claimed internal bankruptcy. This was the *crisis* that was used as the catalyst which allowed for the full transformation of our economy to that of socialism. This fundamental change in philosophy is what laid the foundations to take the United States of America from the most productive, wealthiest nation on planet earth, to the debtor nation she is today. In the process of doing so, it has created wealth beyond comprehension for the select few that have been laying the foundation for the next, up and coming Great Depression.

Whether you are an aspiring politician or just a person that wants to reap huge profits, time is running out for you to benefit from what remains of this particular economic cycle in America. If becoming a politician is your goal and you can find a way to get elected soon, there is still opportunity to amass some personal fortune at the expense of its citizens, but I would suggest you hurry. In the event it is too late for you to take advantage of America's next Great Depression, don't worry. There are other nations to rob and pillage. Become familiar with this recipe to prepare for when that opportunity arises. Keep this in mind, "Success is when opportunity meets preparedness".

What is interesting in America since the government started to embrace socialist policies, is that we started calling depressions, recessions. Nearly all of the recessions from the 1900s to present have been no less severe than what many of our past depressions were in the eighteenth and nineteenth century. Historically, more personal suffrage has been felt on a per capita basis in many of our current recessions than was experienced during most depressions from the pre-socialist era in America. Realistically, America has had several small depressions since the 1930s. As a country, we are now due for what we can only call a "Great Depression". This time, however, the ingredients are in place that will make the depression of the 1930s look like a mild recession by comparison. For all intents and purposes, the American depression makers did a superb job. Their work has paved the road for all those who may be inspired to usurp the wealth of a nation.

2

INGREDIENTS FOR CREATING THE GREATEST OF DEPRESSIONS

In order to create a national depression you will first need to get control of a nation and then you will need to incorporate the following ingredients. I will explain to you how to do both. If you aspire to take over your own nation, you will need to incorporate all of these ingredients. I will both show you what they are and I will give you a guide as to how to implement them in your society. If you are someone that simply wants to grab on to the coattails of an already existing plan, you will want to both understand these ingredients and how they present opportunities for you to jump in and take huge profits at the expense of that nation's citizens.

Disclaimer; these ingredients and this recipe are very specific to both taking over a nation and creating a major depression in order

to create huge personal financial gain. If you do not follow the directions as written, I cannot guarantee that you will get the size or scale of depression that you are looking for to maximize your personal profits.

- ❈ *Taxes:* You will need to impose an income tax on your citizenry in order to create a national depression. Governments that impose income taxes cause depressions.

- ❈ *Borrow:* You will need to borrow money from your citizenry in order to create a national depression. Governments that borrow money cause depressions.

- ❈ *Inflate the currency:* You will need to incorporate inflation in order to create a national depression. Governments that inflate their currency cause the greatest depressions known to man.

- ❈ *Nationalize your banking system:* You will need to nationalize the banks in your nation in order to create a national depression. This is a must! Without nationalizing your nations banking system, you will not be able to create a full-blown across the board national depression and steal the wealth of your nation. Don't skip this part.

- ❈ *Control Interest Rates:* You will need to have control of the interest rates in your nation in order to create a national depression.

- ❈ *Create a currency system based on a philosophy:* This is an important ingredient and a step that cannot be skipped. If you make the mistake and create a currency with something like gold to back it, you will not be able to *inflate* it. This will destroy your chances of creating a super duper "Great Depression" and it will limit the amount of wealth that you are able to pilfer from that society.

These are the only ingredients you will need to create a depression on a national scale, but how you mix the ingredients and get your ingredients into your nation's economy will take careful skill and planning. If you follow this step by step recipe carefully, leaving no steps out, you will be successful at creating a national depression, one that any other depression creator will admire. The road to your depression will deliver phenomenal opportunities to steal the wealth of your citizens and it will create an atmosphere in which they will gladly give you the fruits of their labor.

Get Yourself a Nation

Knowing the necessary ingredients to create a Great Depression is only half the battle. Obviously you are going to need a nation to begin with in order to mix your ingredients. If you have a substantial army, you can probably just go and get yourself a nation. If you can use that method, select a nation that either doesn't have an army or one that is at least not as big as yours. I am going to assume however, that most reading this neither have an army or access to one, but don't let that discourage you. I will show you how to acquire your very own nation (*or at least become part of the team that is already involved in this process in their own nation*), through some simple manipulation. It will require some leg work on your part but hey, "*nothing ventured, nothing gained*". This method of taking over your own nation is a tried and proven method and one that has been used more than once very successfully. If you follow this simple recipe, you will be able to take over and indeed have for both yourself and your future generations your very own nation. I promise! In fact, I guarantee it. Just keep in mind, however, if you don't follow this recipe as I lay it out for you, this guarantee becomes *null and void*.

Find a nation that you would like to take over: The first thing that you will need to do is find a nation. The best nations are ones that have a citizenry that is predominantly *free* and have the right to vote elected officials into government positions. It would be an absolute plus if the nation either has the ability to create, or has already gathered some prior wealth. You really don't want to take over a nation that is in debt. In your search, when you come across those nations that have a lot of debt, you can almost always be assured that someone has beat you to that nation. You will probably have a war on your hands trying to get it for your own. Finding a nation can be an arduous task, but stick with it and just know that it has been done by others very successfully time and time again.

Gain Control of the Government

Here again, if you don't have your own army giving you the ability to simply take over a nation by force, you can accomplish this by allowing special interest groups to financially support you as a candidate for government office. These special interest groups will readily help fund untold propaganda on your behalf. This will assist in getting you elected and all you will need to do is promise to create bills and pass laws that will benefit their personal interests once you have a seat in the government. It's a great trade off for you because it will get you where you need to be in order to create your *depression*. In return you can reward these special interest groups with a portion of the wealth of your nation's citizens, never using a dime of your own money.

Gaining control of the government is not only necessary for the next steps, but as you will soon see, when performed correctly the citizens will not have a clue as to what is taking place. The deception that I will teach you here is extremely important for getting your ingredients into your nation. If the citizens catch on too early, you will not be able to achieve your personal goal and steal their wealth, especially if they are armed.

Another proven method to getting both yourself and your cohorts elected and keeping them elected, would be to find a group of citizens that have a need in your nation. For example, if there is a group of people that are poor or not as well off as some of the others, promise them that you will help support them if they will vote for you and help you and your friends get elected. This is a great way to not only gain political office, but as you set things up in your nation to create your depression, you will actually be able to set up a system that will create many more poor people. This will ensure you're re-elected for years to come. I will show you how you can use your ingredients to not only keep poor people poor, but make lots and lots of poor people. Poor people are vital to your success. The more the better. Don't forget that.

If you don't already, you will need to acquire the ability to stand in front of your nation and lie without flinching. The gift to give eloquent, emotionally charged moving speeches without any real substance is a true art and one that you must practice to become accomplished. I suggest standing in front of the mirror every morning and reciting a list of lies, while keeping a careful eye on your demeanor in the mirror. If you flinch or blink, start from the very beginning again. This is something that should be practiced without fail every single morning before you start your day. Mastering this will deliver untold benefits to you and your accomplices. You will find as you incorporate your ingredients that large groups of the population will simply take you at your word if you can give eloquent speeches. When delivered correctly you will be able to create an atmosphere amongst large groups of people who will cheer you on with tremendous energy without ever investigating for themselves the truth of what you are saying. If you pray, replace your prayer time with this practice. You don't need to be praying if you're doing this anyway. Although, don't stop praying in public. You will need to be able to convince a certain portion of the population that you have some kind of religious belief to obtain their votes. The religion you choose of course depends on the nation you are taking over.

In most nation takeovers, you will need some like-minded friends or accomplices. You will, however, have to offer to share the wealth (some of the spoils if you will), in order to ensure their full cooperation. If your nation operates under the guise of a *representative* type government, similar to that of the United States, with a constitution protecting them from people like you, it will be critical that you recruit a number of accomplices to assist with some necessary alterations and amendments. They can assist you in subtly circumventing that nation's constitution in a manner that the common citizens will remain unaware as it occurs. I will explain how to do that. Not only will I show you how to do that, but I will show you how you can make your citizens actually embrace and support your efforts in making those changes. Isn't this exciting? I can't wait for you to get started.

Change Your Nation's Economic Philosophy

Lay the foundation to change your nation's economic philosophy to socialism

Nations that currently practice socialism already have owners. For this reason, you will want to pick a *free* nation. Of course, if your desire is to stake claim to an existing plan, then you can pick any socialist nation and realize huge profits by understanding this recipe. Socialism is an absolute necessity to claiming ownership of your nation if you don't already have an army to go in and do it for you. In order to create the grandest of all depressions, you must set up a system that will usurp the wealth of your nation and do it in such a way that the common man will be totally unaware of either your intentions or how you are accomplishing this. There is only one proven method to achieving this and it works every single time and that method is *socialism*. Do not stray from this proven philosophy or you will fail and fail miserably. Without socialism, you will not be able to incorporate the ingredients necessary to create a national depression. Reciting this phrase daily will help you to stay focused and on track. *"Freedom and capitalism are my enemy. Freedom and capitalism will prevent me from stealing from my citizens"*. Learn it, know it, live it, in order to guarantee your success.

The first step to laying the foundation for socialism is to get control of the nation's banking system. A national government controlled banking system or even a nationalized privately owned banking system is absolutely essential to successfully converting your nation to the necessary socialist philosophy. Until you can get your hands on the banking system and get total control of the money supply, you simply cannot move on to the next step. Nationalizing your nations banking system is one of the main ingredients in creating your national depression. It is absolutely imperative to mandating inflation, which is another essential ingredient necessary in creating the Grand Daddy of all depressions. If you stay focused and follow these simple steps you will maximize your personal fortunes and create a depression on an unbelievable scale. You will be able to unleash one that any depression creator past or present will truly envy. Here are some helpful tips on both getting your hands on your nation's banks, as well as getting the citizens of your nation to agree to letting you nationalize them.

Never let a good crisis go to waste

This is Nation takeover 101 and one we will talk about many times as you learn how to steal your nation's wealth. ***If a good crisis doesn't present itself, create one.*** As an example, the owners of the United States of America used private bank failures from the early nineteenth century as the crisis to persuade the citizens of its nation to allow them to nationalize their banks. While privately owned capitalist banks from time to time failed, when they did it usually only impacted a segment of society (a local depression), not the nation on a whole. However, there was a handful of bankers in 1907 that through a little well thought out manipulation, created a very large banking crisis in the United States. Those crises were wisely used by these bankers who wanted to steal the wealth of their nation, to persuade the government into convincing the people that it would be in their best interest and indeed the nation's if they controlled and regulated the nations banking systems. These private bankers would both control interest rates as well as the supply of money for the entire nation and they would do it without any interference from the government who by law granted them this power. They created the largest **for profit private central bank** the world has ever seen and these depression creators did this with such success that one hundred years later most Americans still don't know who and what they are. You will need to be cautious here, because there will be a handful of the citizens that know better and you will need to do whatever you can to keep them silent or at least be more persuasive than they are. The point is; crises are your friend. Embrace them and learn how to use them to your favor. If one doesn't present itself to give you the leverage you need to force change then by all means create one.

Always remember to play on the people's general good nature when convincing them to go along with something that only you know will ultimately be their ruin. Your goal as you mix your ingredients should be to dumb down the population of your nation. You must create a level of deception that will not only be invisible to the common man, but will foster an environment in which he will endorse the very things that will bring about his own demise.

Take for instance the method cattle ranchers use to slaughter their herds. They do this in such a way that the cattle line up for slaughter without ever getting nervous or skittish as they approach their moment of death. The ranchers know if the cattle get anxious, that it will send adrenaline through their bodies and toughen the meat. To prevent this, they corral the herd into gates that force them to line up in single file so that they cannot see what is happening to the cows in front of them. One of our ingredients, inflation, will create a deception no less effective. Nationalizing your nation's banks is necessary to creating inflation. Creating a variety of deceptions with your ingredients is easy and will help you steal your nation's wealth without even the best educated becoming aware of it before the deed is done.

Impose an Income Tax

An income tax imposed on the citizens of a nation will always cause a depression. Imposing an income tax and using the money obtained to both support areas of your nation's economy that are not producing (*due to normal economic conditions*) and by giving that money to the portion of the society that is non-productive (*not supporting themselves or produce anything*), will help to get your nation on a solid path towards socialism and the eventual depression you are looking to create.

Simply by taking from the productive sector through taxation and handing that money out to the nonproductive sector will help you to expedite the process of overturning your nation's existing society. If you follow these instructions, you will be able to create false boom cycles (*the business cycle*) in areas of the economy that you select to stimulate (*spend the tax money*) time and time again. Equally important, once you implement both the income tax and the socialist philosophy of priming (*spending the tax money*) in certain areas of the economy, you can now start to extract profit from this process for both you and your cohorts.

Through the manipulation of spending the tax money, you can now pay back your special interest supporters by passing laws that grant them these taxed funds to support their own interests. You will be able to create hundreds of opportunities allowing you to line their pockets with your citizen's tax dollars. Not only that, but now you can do things like, force stock prices to go up by granting particular companies your citizen's funds.

You will want to make sure that you and your friends make your personal investments in these companies prior to giving them the taxpayers' dollars. Some of the best methods are to invest in companies that supply goods and services to the companies you are giving your citizens tax dollars too. This way you can keep your private investments well hidden and few if any of your citizens will be able to tie back your investments directly to the companies your government is supporting. This way you can all realize huge financial gains by inflating a variety of stock prices. You can even deliver this *insider information* to a number of other people, preferably ones who will be able to help further your cause, lining their pockets with inflated stocks at the expense of the other unknowing stockholders. This will keep people in your back pocket that will end up owing you huge personal favors for assisting them in acquiring massive fortunes at your citizen's expense.

If you implement these ingredients, over the years, you, your cohorts and future generations to follow will be able to enter public office with little or no money and steal vast amounts of wealth from your nation. The real beauty of this when performed correctly is that your citizens will unknowingly assist you in implementing your ingredients that will allow you to steal from them.

The areas in which you spend the tax money in your economy will create a temporary boom in the *business cycle*, but this boom will eventually wear off and a recession or a depression will occur if you do not spend more money (*stimulus*) in that same area of the economy to keep it going. So what you will want to do is tax more and spend more at an increasing rate in order to continue to support that part of the economy. This will require raising taxes to keep things going so that you and your friends can continue to manipulate the economy and create opportunities to steal from your citizens.

At the same time, you will want to use a portion of the taxes you impose to insure that you remain in office. You will want to give a portion of the tax money to support the citizens that belong to the segment of your society that is nonproductive. This will make them both dependent on you and your government and content with just surviving. They will be in your corner and remain there for as long as you give them money to support themselves. If you implement this plan correctly, you will be able to get people who work for a living but whose incomes are close to what you are giving away, to quit their jobs and join the portion of society that you are supporting. This way they too will endorse and vote for you in future elections.

The more marginally poor people you can get to depend on a portion of the money you are taking from the productive tax-paying citizens, the more this will help to secure your standing in your government for a very long time. What is great about an income tax is while you tax your working citizens, you will be able to take those who have incomes comparable to the ones your government is taking care of, and tax them right into the same poverty level. With a little luck, many of those citizens will simply give up working and allow you to transfer yet more wealth from the productive sector to the nonproductive sector, making even more people dependent on you. This too will increase your voting base substantially over time. You must be cautious however, because if you tax your productive citizens too fast, the risk of them catching on to what you are doing increases and you will need to stop for a period of time. Your ultimate goal should be to create a system that will both create a poverty class dependent on your government and one that will serve to keep them there. Imposing taxes will help you to accomplish this relatively easily. There is a balance that you must strike between your productive class and your nonproductive class as you implement these ingredients. There is a risk if you haven't reached the point yet in your nation's economy were you have enough dependent voters, that the tax-paying citizen may catch on to your scheme and make you stop. If this happens, the areas you spent their money will suffer a certain depression, one premature to achieving one on the scale you really want. This will only serve to irritate your citizens to the point that they vote you out of office, and you will lose the opportunity to control the nation and steal greater wealth for yourself and your accomplices.

If you happen to take over a nation whose philosophies and concepts do not support an income tax, you will want to change that immediately. A nation that does not allow taxing their citizen's income will prevent you from stealing their wealth. For example: The American socialist when laying their plan, understood the importance of taxing the income of their citizens. Prior to 1913, the government from time to time toyed with a progressive tax on its citizen's income but met resistance and lost those battles. Americans in the eighteenth and nineteenth centuries knew all too well that the only way to control government and prevent it from growing to the point that it would infringe on personal freedom, was to limit its financial resources. This all changed however during the Woodrow Wilson administration when three fourths of the states ratified the 16th amendment and when congress enacted the *Revenue act of 1913*. Imposing an income tax is vital to both a nation take over and usurping the wealth of your citizens. Without an income tax, you will not be able to redistribute your citizen's wealth or grow your government, making it virtually impossible to create the dependency necessary to accomplish your plan.

To obtain a great level of success, you must strike a balance of taxing at a rate which at first will appear tolerable to the taxpayer base, while growing your non-taxpayer dependent base. If you are successful at getting some of the other ingredients into the pot, it will help you to both tax your taxpayers and even your non-taxpayers in a manner that they won't even see or understand what is happening to them. This will help to soften the blow and keep your goals both hidden and on track while at the same time ensuring a long run stealing the wealth of your nation.

If taxes are the only ingredient you can muster up, imposing an income tax and the method by which you spend those taxed dollars *will* create a depression. Over time, you will be able to expand the nonproductive sector of your economy and reduce the productive sector by relieving them of a portion of their wealth. However, if you want to expand your depression to a *catastrophic* level and steal the wealth at a greater rate, you must include these other key ingredients.

CREATE GOVERNMENT BORROWING

Government borrowing will cause a depression. It is both a historical and mathematical fact and an ingredient you absolutely want to incorporate into your recipe. Get your government to borrow and you will be able to steal more wealth and do it in a manner in which the people will not know or feel that they are getting taxed as much. Use this as a tool for when you see your citizens becoming uncomfortable with paying higher taxes. Government borrowing is a concept that will guarantee a *national depression.* It will serve to increase the level of wealth that you can extract from your current citizens while at the same time extracting the wealth from the unborn future generations. Borrowing will allow you the ability to financially enslave an entire society that hasn't even arrived yet.

If you implement this ingredient correctly, it will enable you to borrow from your nation's citizens and demand that your citizens be responsible for paying themselves back with interest. Isn't that great? Think about it. You go to a friend and ask to borrow a hundred dollars, you then tell your friend that he owes you a hundred dollars with interest so that you can pay him back. I know, stop laughing! People around you might catch on and we can't have everyone doing this. There simply are not enough nations to go around. If our friend is ignorant enough to go for this, we can continue to borrow from him and have him pay himself back for those loans he made to us. We can continue this process with him until he simply runs out of money and suffers his own personal depression.

Once you incorporate borrowing into your nation's economy, you can use it to balance the amount you tax from your people against the amount that you borrow from them. When you notice that your citizens are getting a little antsy over their tax burden, simply borrow more instead of raising taxes. They won't notice this at first, because you will make payments using their money against what you borrowed from them in small increments and in effect put the debt burden off to a period in the future making their kids and future generations for years to come pay for it. Best case scenario, you can borrow money and only pay the interest on the money owed just simply raising your nation's debt as you steal its future wealth.

If you can continue to drive your nation into debt and use the money borrowed to increase your own personal wealth (spend the borrowed money like you would in the *tax section*), then never pay that debt off, when your depression occurs it will become a huge win for you and your associates. However, you have to be careful. As the payments come due on the money your government borrows, you will either have to borrow more or tax more to pay back what you have borrowed. You can't miss a payment because you will risk the tax-paying citizens catching on. If you lose the ability to borrow and tax more, than your nation will suffer a depression which may be premature if you haven't thoroughly robbed them of all their future wealth.

The ideal situation would be to get your citizens to believe that debt is necessary for the nation to succeed and there may just be a slim chance that they won't even require your government to get permission to borrow more and more money as time goes on. In that case, you can simply just run wild with stealing all of their future wealth very quickly. It would be prudent though to have patience and work things in a manner that will allow a certain portion of your citizens to continue to create wealth, so that there is more to steal in the long run. Look at the long term. Greed is good, but temper it with patience so you can maximize your greed.

To get started borrowing, your government will have to produce debt instruments (ways to borrow money from your citizens) to sell to the public that bear an interest rate at a level that will encourage your people to purchase them (lend your government their money).

For Example; some of the most notable forms of government borrowing would be how the United States of America borrows from its citizens. They use what is commonly referred to as both long and short term debt instruments such as Treasury bills or T-bills. They have used Savings Bonds and other methods along the way as well. They place an interest rate on these T-bills or government securities that will encourage their citizens to purchase them (lend them money) as an investment. When their government needs to borrow more money (because it can no longer tax without putting their political careers in peril), they simply raise the amount of money (interest rates) they are willing to pay their citizens in order to entice a greater number of people and corporations to lend them more money. Today, many investment firms, money market funds, retirement funds, hedge funds and private equity firms lend money to their government (purchase T-bills) as an investment when the government is offering a higher rate of return (interest rate) than they can get from a bank or other investment sources. Since their government only has three ways of generating revenue, *taxing, borrowing* or *inflating,* the government borrows from the wealth of its citizens with interest, and then either taxes or *borrows* from its citizens in order to pay themselves back. When they can't *tax or borrow* the money they *inflate* it. In this case, they borrow from their citizens with interest and pay them back with dollars that are worth less than the ones they originally borrowed from them. Gotta love it!

You will have to attempt to strike a balance between how much you tax your citizens and how much you borrow. Between what you and your cohorts steal off the top coupled with stimulating your special interest groups to keep them going, holding off your great depression is a fine balancing act until you have stolen all the nation's wealth. As you raise interest rates in order to borrow more, you risk that other businesses in the economy will lose the ability to borrow capital to keep their business going. This occurs when the banks they use cannot borrow money at a low enough interest rate so that they can turn around and lend it out to them and make a profit. If the banks cannot compete with the interest rates that your government is offering to borrow money from your citizens, this can and will cause your economy to slow and indeed suffer a depression. One most likely that will be premature to you stealing everything you can from the nation. There are some great regulations you can put in place that will allow you to raise interest rates so that your government can continue to borrow, while at the same time expanding the credit supply so that your banks can continue to lend. These regulations will ensure that there is enough credit available at the local banks allowing businesses to go into debt in order to produce, and it will allow your citizens to go further into debt in order to consume.

While the creation of currency out of thin air is one way of implementing *inflation* in your nation, you can also use the nationalized banking system to inflate the credit supply. As you steal the available wealth (the savings) from your nation, the expansion of credit will become imperative to keeping your nation producing and consuming giving you the ability to steal away the majority of their future wealth. As your nations current wealth is transferred to you and your cohorts, credit will be the only thing that will keep the nation going. Through your nationalized central banking system, you will be able to control the expansion of credit in your nation. This alone will allow you to steal beyond most peoples comprehension. It will allow you to steal any possible wealth from those that haven't even been conceived yet well off into the future.

Once again, the American socialists mastered this technique and you should both study it and use it while creating your road to a great depression. The American socialist ensured consumer debt by creating a nifty trick in accounting called "**fractional reserving**". This is an area that you will want to pay close attention to, because this little trick will allow you to transfer your nations wealth in a very subtle and unique manner.

When the American socialist started to implement their plan, they were faced with a nation in which the banks operated on what was commonly referred to as *"Sound Banking Practices"*. It is important for you to understand what those are, so if you come across them you can take measures to stop them. Sound banking practices will prevent you from stealing the future wealth of your nation.

Before 1913, banks in America would take in money in the form of deposits made by consumers who wanted to make money by investing (*saving*) it in these banking institutions. These types of deposits used to be called *"time deposits"*. These deposits are held by the banking institution for a set amount of time and the bank paid their investors (depositors) a specific amount of money (interest), for leaving their money with them. The banker could then turn around and lend that money out to other people and businesses for a variety of reasons. This allowed the bankers to lend money at a specific interest rate. One that would cover the interest the bankers paid for these *time deposits*, the banks *business expenses*, and then left a small amount for the *bank's profit*. The surprising thing about those bankers was that they knew they couldn't lend out more money than they received in the form of *time deposits*.

The citizens of this nation would also put money in those banks that they wanted to use to purchase goods and services by using bank notes. These types of accounts are called *demand deposits*, because the people that put their money in these types of accounts could *demand* it back at any time they wished. The bankers would issue bank notes (similar to the checks we are issued today) so that people that had these types of deposits could give their bank notes to merchants when they made purchases. The merchants could then take those notes to the issuing bank and trade them for a portion of the deposits held there on behalf of the person who gave them the bank notes. Unlike paying an *interest* like they did for *time deposits,* banks charged a fee for this service as a convenience to both the depositor and the merchants they did business with. Banks knew that they couldn't make loans against *demand deposits* simply because they had no idea or guarantee as to how long they would have those funds in their bank. Bankers back then operated under the philosophy that they could not lend out money that they didn't have.

This is a philosophy that if followed in your nation will need to be changed, and changed quickly. It is absolutely contrary to what your banks will need to do, and if *sound banking practices* are allowed to remain in effect, they will keep you from stealing much of your nation's wealth.

As the American socialist implemented the act of borrowing money from its citizens to increase government spending, they had to offer a higher interest rate than banks could offer for time deposits. This put an obvious crunch on the amount of capital the banks could take in, causing a ripple effect as to how much they could lend out. As the economy became debt driven due to government intervention, this government created phenomenon became detrimental to the American socialist plan. It would create a situation in which the economy would start to go into a *recession* or a *depression,* if the citizens of their nation did not have access to more debt. The American socialist, being the brilliant thieves that they are, created a number of banking regulations to both mask the effects of their borrowing and *inflate* the credit supply. Today, this concept, and in fact government imposed regulation on behalf of the privately owned central bank the Federal Reserve is called *fractional reserving*.

Fractional reserving allows banks to lend out many more times the amount of money than what they hold in actual reserves. Through tricks in accounting, banks today can lend multiple times the amount that they take into their banks in the form of time deposits. While the *fractional reserve rate* dictated by the Federal Reserve will vary, today banks can usually lend out 8 to 10 times more money than they hold in reserves under this nifty banking regulation. Not only can they lend more than they take in, but they can use *demand deposits* (money people put in checking accounts) as part of their *reported reserves* against the loans that they make. They can do this even though they have no way of knowing how long they will have those funds. Today, the majority of *savings accounts* in America are not even *time deposits*. They have become *demand deposits*, allowing people the ability to demand their savings at anytime. Through *fractional reserving*, the American socialist found a way to usurp most of the available investment capital from the citizens of the nation while at the same time inflating the credit supply. As a result, these banking practices coupled with the Federal Reserves ability to print currency have diminished the purchasing power year over year of their citizens. Through this method the private bankers have been able to reduce each year a percentage of the citizen's wealth without them becoming aware of it.

To prevent the general public from realizing the full impact of taxation and borrowing, you need to incorporate an ingredient that I have already alluded to: *inflation*.

Inflate Your Currency

If you thought borrowing from your citizens and getting them to pay back the money they loan you was ingenious, you are going to love what *inflation* will do for your plan. Once again, in order to implement this ingredient, you must have nationalized your nation's banking system and have total control of the money supply. Stay focused here because this is critical to increasing your profits while you steal the wealth of your nation. Inflation is the one ingredient that is critical to stealing huge amounts of your nations wealth. In fact if you could only use one ingredient for your plan, this is the one you should choose. I can not stress enough how important inflation is to your success. Every successful nation thief understands the importance of inflation in their recipe. You must protect it, nurture it and above all do whatever it takes to prevent any members of your nation from stopping it once you incorporate it. If you can successfully balance *taxation, borrowing* and *inflation* for a period of time, you will have a powerful recipe for a *catastrophic* depression. These three ingredients will allow you to successfully enslave the entire population's labor over time. They will support you and actually call for the policies and regulations that you want to impose upon them. They will do this at an ever increasing rate until your depression roars into full swing. Once that occurs, many of them will awaken from their slumber and realize what you did to them, but it will be way too late. They will hate you, but they will realize that you are now a necessary evil in their lives. They will chirp like little birdies in a nest with their beaks pointed high in the air begging for any little crumb you are willing to share with them. (Provided of course that they are not armed, but we will discuss how to take care of that issue later).

Inflation is the act of printing currency with nothing but a philosophy to back it. In other words, if you need more money you fire up the printing presses and print more money. The end result of printing more money is that it will devalue both the new money and the old money in effect making it worth less. This will cause all other things in your nation's economy to increase in price. It's not that all those other things are actually going up in price because they are becoming more valuable, it is simply taking more of the newly printed devalued dollars to purchase them.

The benefit to you is that when you print the money, you use it to cover any spending that you couldn't tax or borrow and since you are the creator of the inflation, you reap the most benefits. The majority of the devaluation isn't realized until it trickles down to your citizens. This tool will allow you to spend at a much higher rate than ever before. Remember, your goal is to spend as much as possible. Spending will serve to control the economy allowing both you and your cohorts the ability to pillage from the public and amass great personal wealth. At the same time, spending will help you grow the poor dependent sector in order to ensure that you stay secure in your position. Spend, spend, spend, the end result will be that ever so subtly, over a period of time, you will reduce the wealth of your citizens, creating an environment in which it will cost them more to survive. They will seldom if ever blame this on you, because inflation will hide that fact. It just becomes a normal occurrence of life to them. When they walk into a store to buy a gallon of milk and that gallon has gone up a dime, or when a loaf of bread increases a nickel in price, they will never understand that you are the reason for that. They will all think that the milk and the bread has gone up in value never understanding that it has not. It just takes more of their devalued dollars for them to purchase the milk and bread. As time goes on they will get use to prices going up on everything they need to survive while you steal their ability to maintain their lifestyles, never realizing for a moment what inflation is and how you are using it to grow your government. What is so incredibly cool about the ingredient inflation, as time goes on and future generations are born into your system, it will be a normal way of life for them. They won't even think to question either you or your future generations that you leave your system too. It will simply be the *"new norm"* so to speak. The masses will actually fall into a slumber of ignorance which will work in your favor for as long as you and yours continue to inflate their currency.

Once you get inflation incorporated into your plan, you will have the ability to create money to cover your spending when borrowing and taxing become politically unfeasible. You will be able to steal your nation's wealth by taxing, borrowing and inflating. You will truly have the best three ingredients for creating a national depression.

Like Busy Bees

Another beautiful part about inflation is the chaos it will cause amongst both the citizens and the politicians in your nation. They will be like busy bees for years trying to cure all the problems that will crop up in their economy, never stopping to understand that these economic ills are the *effects* of you inflating the currency they use. It is a sure way to keep the politicians that aren't part of your crew out of your business while you steal the nation's wealth. In fact, they are apt to be so busy passing new laws and regulations in response to what the inflation will do to the economy, that there will be very little risk of any of them ever stopping long enough to step back and attempt to see what you are doing. Inflation coupled with a few handy socialist programs (that we will review in later chapters), will allow you to totally dumb down the entire population of your nation to the point that if anyone figures out what you're doing, the rest of the population will simply not believe them. When incorporated into your plan correctly, a percentage of your citizens will start to blame the effects of this on everyone other than you. They will blame it on people who have more wealth than they do, they will blame it on companies that make profits, they will blame it on the smaller bankers, the investors, oil companies, farmers, big business, small business and the list will go on and on. The point is, they will spend their time placing the blame on everyone other than the *real* cause of this situation, which is you inflating the currency!

If you get all the ingredients incorporated into your nation, the chaos it will create will become so rampant that your society will splinter into groups that will assist you in stealing from them. Both your citizens and the politicians in your government, will neatly divide themselves up in groups opposing each other at any cost. Individualism will by and large cease to exist at every level. People will give up their ability to think for themselves in favor of agreeing with an agenda put forth by just a few individuals that control their group. You will be able to measure your success by how well divided your society becomes.

Once you get these six steps implemented into your nation's economy, you will be on your way to massive opportunities for you, your family and any members of your inner circle. You will be able to achieve the fortunes only possible by enslaving the labor of a nation. However, your work is not over. You now have to manipulate the system using your ingredients to maximize your profits.

There are certain things you can do to either accelerate the road to your depression or slow it down if you need more time to usurp more wealth from the population. You are also going to have to do some careful planning and controlling to ensure that the majority of your citizens starts to turn to you as their means of survival. Your goal at this point is to make the entire economy of your nation dependent for its very survival on the amount of money that your government is willing to spend to keep it going. In fact, as you approach this end, you can use this as an indicator as to how close you are to creating your massive depression. If manipulated correctly, you can have years and years of accumulating wealth for you and anyone else you choose at the expense of your nation's citizens. It will be important however to both keep your citizens busy creating more wealth for you to steal, while at the same time implementing policies that will gradually reduce their knowledge and common sense. In fact, you will be able to create an entire nation who will willingly surrender their ability to comprehend what you are doing to them. While this might sound at first a daunting task, I assure you that it can and has been done and I will gladly show you how to accomplish this. Once again, it requires some tenacity, but hey, it will ensure unimaginable profits.

3

Dumbing Down Your Nation

The very last thing you want is a population that has the intelligence to see what you are doing. After all, your success at this point is going to be dependent on NOT GETTING CAUGHT! Fortunately, there are steps that I will show you that will ensure that you can dumb down your citizens. If you are taking over a nation in which the people are fairly intelligent to begin with, there are proven methods that when put in place will serve to reverse that trend. Once again, the more people you can make dependent on you and your government the easier stealing from them will become.

While you can start with a nation founded upon self-reliance and sound business practices, your goal is going to be to reverse that trend. Equally, the last thing you want is a bunch of financial wizards running around in your nations business. While simply incorporating the six ingredients in this recipe will serve to jump start your nation on the path to economic dependency and ruin, you will have to implement some social programs that will reduce the level of awareness throughout your society in order to maximize your thievery. For example, if you started with a nation in which families work to increase their individual wealth for both themselves and for their future generations, you are going to want to put a stop to that. People who do that continue to become more educated and more self-reliant. If this behavior is allowed to occur on a large scale, it will most certainly make difficult, if not impossible your pursuit to steal that nation's wealth. Thankfully there are proven methods to reverse those kinds of trends in a society and indeed prevent it from occurring on any type of scale that would become a threat to yourself or your government.

There are basically two methods by which people gain knowledge and become more educated and aware. The obvious one is what I like to call the *scholastic method*. This is a method by which people gain knowledge from others via books, schools, and other materials based on both past and present experiences and studies. The second method is what I call *knowledge through evolution*. This is the type of knowledge that people obtain as their lives evolve. This would include the challenges they come across in their day to day living and how they learn to overcome those challenges. While there are ways to control the scholastic method via controlling what is written, taught and available, the area of knowledge that you will be able to easily curtail is knowledge through evolution. By the simple act of implementing inflation and regulations into your nation, you will be able to start to reduce the level of knowledge and awareness amongst your citizens over time. This will allow you to deceive them at the rate necessary to steal their wealth.

Here is one example: In the United States of America, prior to the American socialist implementing their plan to accomplish their goals, the country was plagued with a population who lived according to the belief that families should stay together, work together and create wealth together. This radical way of thinking caused most of the population to prefer *independence* and *freedom* over any type of government intervention. Well, I don't have to tell you how those kinds of values simply will not work in order for you to take control of the population and steal their wealth. Those, whose goals were clearly set on stealing the wealth of America, possessed a keen awareness of this as well. So when they took the six steps listed in this recipe, they also instituted a variety of programs that by design allowed for a government takeover of certain areas of what was normally considered a citizen's personal responsibility. These programs overtime would change those core values and they worked magnificently!

The American socialist instituted programs and regulations that in time totally reversed many of the core beliefs of it citizens. Not only did they put them into reverse for the population of that time, but they diminished the ability for future generations to continue to progress by learning things for themselves through life experiences. Of course the American Socialist (specifically those in the Franklin Delano Roosevelt administration) knew that they couldn't simply institute these programs without gaining the agreement from at least most of the current citizens. A plan was needed to gain this approval.

The American socialist learned quickly to **never let a good crisis go to waste**. The Great Depression created a number of quick short term crises that the Roosevelt Administration used to talk the nation into the many changes ushered in under Roosevelt's *"New Deal"*. From the implementation of *Social Security*, using a small part of the population that never planned for their own retirement as an excuse, to the creation of *welfare* and *inflating the currency,* the "Roosevelt era" brought about a great number of both social and economic reforms to America. Many of these reforms sold under the guise of a "New Deal", created reforms necessary for the privately owned Federal Reserve (the wealthy bankers) to both control, and reduce the wealth of the citizens of this nation. Roosevelt also learned at this time how to use the media to pull on the heart strings of the good natured American people. Just as is done today, his clever use of the media was vital to convincing the public into accepting the changes needed for instituting his socialist plans. These changes have been the catalyst that have allowed for the takeover of both the citizen's wealth and their sense of responsibility over to the wealthiest bankers and the United States government.

In the 1930s, President Franklin Delano Roosevelt pioneered the use of the media to put pressure on the United States congress to support bills they would not otherwise support. Roosevelt started using the radio to address the nation in what was coined the *"fireside chats."* Roosevelt used these radio addresses to both convince the citizens that certain programs were required for the overall health of the nation and to put pressure on Congress to pass the progressive socialist agenda. After these fireside chats, letters from the listening population would come pouring into congress, putting pressure on those who would otherwise not endorse such socialist policies to vote for them. Roosevelt and his cohorts learned quickly to **never let a good crisis go to waste** in order to promote their socialist agenda.

In 1935, a program that was part of Roosevelt's "New Deal" (gotta love that phrase), was implemented. It was and is to this day called the Social Security System. Now stay with me here because this is an important lesson for those who want to take over and steal a nation's wealth.

Prior to the Social Security System, the citizens had that nasty habit of taking care of their own, coupled with the crazy habit of creating wealth from generation to generation. As stated earlier, this would not fare well if you want to steal the wealth of a nation. Always remember that dependency is crucial to stealing a nation's wealth. If the population continued to be *independent*, overtime they would learn how to create and save wealth. History supports that for the first 150 years of this independent *capitalist* philosophy, the American population created more wealth than any other nation of people on planet earth. If left alone, they would be prone to learning through both their scholastic studies and their individual mistakes and people would continue to learn from each other the best ways to ensure their financial security. It would keep in place a learning process incorporated at their founding, which would allow most members of the society to make personal progress. While not every single member of society would be successful, this environment would allow the vast majority of people the opportunity to advance, gain knowledge and accumulate wealth for generations. During those times, there weren't any retirement homes because families took care of families. It allowed young members of a family to learn from previous generations and it instilled a sense of both self and family responsibility across the nation.

For socialism to take hold allowing them to steal their nation's wealth, this philosophy had to change and change drastically. Through the use of the then mass media, the American socialists were able to manipulate the nation. They convinced the people to write their political leaders and encourage them to accept the change that would allow them to turn over their wealth and indeed their morals and sense of responsibility to the American Social Security System.

Social Security removed the need for the citizens of this nation to be as concerned with taking personal responsibility in planning for their futures. The majority of Americans from that era, especially the younger ones believed (because they had been told by the American socialists), that the investment they were forced to pay into for Social Security by law, would be there for them in their old age. Therefore, the need to continue to learn the fundamentals of investing, saving and budgeting for the future, along with the need for making prudent financial decisions for the long term; such as building and passing wealth from generation to generation, or continuing to take care of aging generations within the family unit, all diminished. Social Security served to destroy the traditional family fiber in

America. It cleared the way to making an entire segment of the American population dependent on the government. At the same time, it reduced the level of knowledge and education amongst an entire population historically obtained through the *natural laws of evolution*.

If you implement this type of program into your plan to steal your nation's wealth, if you follow the same road map that the American socialist did, by law, you can take the money citizens are forced to pay into the Social Security fund and spend it. This will allow you to steal more of the nation's wealth for yourself and your accomplices. It's a shrewd plan and I highly suggest using this very same proven model. Today, it is called an *"entitlement"* program in which the taxpayers are on the hook over and above what they pay into it since the government spent all the money on other wealth usurping programs. Another great benefit of social security is that the American socialist can now use the threat of reducing or even eliminating the payments owed to the older generation as a means to secure more votes. You have to see the beauty in that!

While I suggest you model your plan based on the same Social Security program that destroyed the family fiber and made a huge segment of the population dependent in America, you still have other segments that you will have to engage to make those areas dependent as well. Here again, the American socialist model has some great tried-and-proven programs that will allow you to create tremendous dependency and will ultimately serve to keep the general population from gaining the knowledge necessary to both better themselves or hinder your plan.

The American Welfare system is one that is well worth adopting and will guarantee you maximum personal profits. It will ensure a huge number of voters will keep you in the right position to continue to pilfer and pillage from them. The Welfare program instituted by the American socialist will guarantee a level of poverty that will continue to grow over time. It will absolutely keep a very large portion of your citizens totally ignorant to what you are doing to them. When implemented correctly, a great percentage of the population that you net into poverty and keep there for generations, will by-and-large lose their ability to gain *intelligence through evolution* at a rate beyond imagination.

While passed under the guise of a safety net to prevent folks from falling into the depths of poverty, it is the perfect program to draw people into poverty with a guarantee of keeping them there once you catch them. It is a beautiful program and once again one that you should implement into your plan. I would caution you though; there will be a group of people that will want to put limits or indeed control this program attempting to make it a stepping stone for getting people up and out of poverty. These people will try to encourage your poor people into becoming productive citizens by way of limiting the amount of time they can spend in the net. You must do everything you can to prevent that from happening. It is imperative that you have a system that from the outside, gives the population the appearance of doing just that, but in reality makes people poor and once you catch them in the "net", keeps them there forever. A few may escape but don't fret over that. As long as the vast majority can't escape it, then you have successfully accomplished the intended goal. Once again, I suggest the American welfare model to guarantee your success.

Those are just a couple but not all of the social programs that I highly recommend you incorporate into your plan. These programs will absolutely guarantee your personal success in your pursuit to steal your nation's wealth. It will guarantee that your nation will have a Great depression. History will indeed remember and talk about your depression for years to come. Just think; others in the future will be able to look at what you have done and use your model when they too want to steal the wealth and enslave an entire nation.

4

KEEP YOUR NATION BUSY

"Idle hands are the devils workshop"

Once your plan is in place and has taken root, you will need to protect it by keeping your nation busy. The last thing you want at this point is for your deceit and thievery to come to light. You must spend some of your time and attention to ensure that the chances of your citizens discovering your plan never occur. Remember, if they discover the plan and are able to see it for what it is, not only will you lose the ability to continue to steal from them, but if the citizens of your nation are armed, your very life and that of your co-conspirators could end up being in grave danger.

The ingredient *inflation* that you incorporated into your plan will keep both the politicians and members of your society extremely busy. They will spend untold years trying to fix the effects of your inflation, without it ever occurring to them to simply stop you from doing it. What you clearly will have on your side as you steal your nations wealth is that inflation alone will keep your politicians, lawyers and your educators busy coming up with laws, regulations and social policies all with the intent of resolving the *"effects"* that inflation is guaranteed to create. It will ensure that your judicial system is swamped, spending the majority of its time measuring and weighing against any constitution, the thousands of new laws and regulations created to stop the effects of inflation. The measure of its insanity will be no less than that of the little Dutch Boy, who attempts to stop a leak in the dam by putting his finger in the hole. Once he plugs one, another appears and then another and another, until he has no fingers left to cover all the leaks. Inflation will have this exact same effect on all of the policy makers, educators, lawyers, CEO's, investing consultants, local bankers, business owners and just about anyone in your society whose intelligence might otherwise get in the way of your plan.

You should encourage this behavior by stirring the pot from time to time. You will want to encourage division amongst your citizens. Divide them into groups that have differing opinions on how your government should spend its money in order to cure the very things that inflation is creating. Dividing your nation will bring untold fortunes to you as long as neither group stops you from spending. If integrated correctly, you can create a political atmosphere in which it appears to the citizens that they have a choice of two very different viewpoints, when in actuality both of those viewpoints (provided they don't stop inflation) will support your philosophy of socialism.

Encourage these groups and, if possible, find ways to fund them to keep them going. Through a little encouragement, you will be able to create an environment in which your citizens will stay constantly busy and confused, disagreeing with each other on literally thousands of issues all created by your inflation. Not only will the majority of their time be focused on each other, but in their pursuit to impose their differing opinions on each other, they will actually aid you in passing laws and regulations which will expedite your ability to steal and enslave them. It's a win, win for you either way it goes.

You and your government should find ways to get these various groups to focus on social issues versus economic issues. For example, the American socialist became experts on keeping their citizens focused and dividing themselves over issues like who can marry who, if a woman had a right to have an abortion, or if any reference of God should be allowed in public places. Like sleight of hand from a magician, there are literally hundreds of things that you can condition your citizens to focus on in order to prevent them from seeing your plan. You will want to pay some attention to the numbers of people who have a common belief in all these issues. This will help you to understand how to use those numbers to help keep members of your government elected.

Practice changing your opinion like the wind so that you can take full advantage of the most popular group's beliefs at the time. You must become an expert in making the appropriate promises to them in order to gain their votes at election time. Of course, this doesn't mean you have to fulfill any promises made.

To the contrary, with just a little work on your part, you can make huge promises and once the election is over, you can use the excuse that members from the opposing party prevented you from keeping your promises. You will be able to play this same scenario over and over again, and your citizens will never get tired of it. More often than not, it will firm up their resolve to oppose each other at an ever increasing rate, spawning the confusion required to keep your plan in place.

Extracting the Wealth of Your Nation

"There is no subtler, no surer means of overturning the existing basis of society than to debauch the currency. This process engages all the hidden forces of economic law on the side of destruction, and does it in a manner which not one man in a million is able to diagnose". -Vladimir Lenin

Inflation, taxing, and borrowing will present several opportunities for you to extract the wealth of your nation. Inflation by itself is the one ingredient that will allow you to expand your government and create huge profits for yourself and your accomplices without the general public becoming aware of your plan. This section will teach you how to make huge personal profits while your government ever-so-subtly takes over full control of your nation's economy. You will learn how to usurp not just the personal wealth of your citizens, but if you follow this recipe, you will successfully take over all of your nation's natural resources as well. You will learn how to completely take control of your nations manufacturing, all of the personal property, public lands, gas, oil, food, health care and all of your citizen's labor. You will be able to effectively reverse your citizen's concept from savings as a measure of both personal and national wealth to debt being the new measure. This concept reversal is paramount to your ultimate success.

Obviously, controlling a government that controls a nation's economy will allow you to make huge personal profits at the citizen's expense. However, the ultimate goal is for your government to take total control over every aspect of your citizen's lives. It's one thing to steal the wealth that your nation currently possesses when you implement your plan. It is quite another to be able to steal the wealth for many years into the future. Over time, your plan is going to diminish the wealth available for you to take, so it is imperative that you put in place a plan that will allow you to steal the future wealth of the inhabitants of your nation for generations to come.

Reverse the Concept of Savings and Debt

If the nation you are taking over starts off with savings and wealth, it is probably brimming with citizens who have a concept that savings, property ownership and personal possessions are the measurement of their wealth.

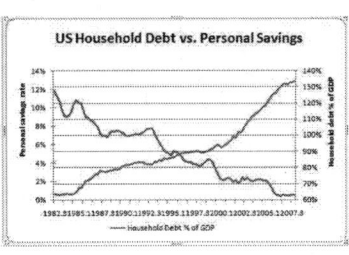

Savings vs Debt

This is a concept that you must change in order to maximize your ability to steal from both the current population and the future generations in your nation. Changing this concept will allow you to line the pockets of both you and your associates today, while forcing future generations to pay for what you have stolen for years into the future. It will also guarantee that future generations are enslaved to insurmountable debt making them in effect slaves to your government while paying you and your government back for the wealth you stole from them. While changing the perception that savings measures wealth, to that of debt measuring wealth, may seem an insurmountable task, it is an achievable one and relatively easy to do.

When the American socialist implemented their plan on their nation, its citizens had a solid belief that *savings* was imperative to increasing ones wealth. Conversely, there was a common belief amongst the population that *debt* was the opposite of *savings* and indeed the very opposite of *wealth*. If this core belief was allowed to run rampant, the American socialist would be limited to what they could steal for both themselves as well as limiting what their future generations would be able to steal.

What ultimately would happen is that they could steal the existing wealth, but then the *jig* would be up and their *depression* would take place. This would eliminate their ability to steal anything further until the nation recovered and created more wealth.

There would be great risk as well, because a premature depression might bring their plan to light, waking up their citizens. This would prevent them from stealing any future wealth and quite possibly keep them from stealing their wealth ever again. You can see how this *savings equals wealth* concept would have stood firmly in the way of their plan. Changing this concept takes a bit of time, but fortunately, all the necessary ingredients were in place that ensured the reversal of this concept.

The American socialist understood, that there were only three ways for their government to gain revenue: taxing, borrowing and inflating. They knew that these three government revenue generators would lay the foundation to alter the *savings* to *wealth* concept for the entire nation. As they stole the available wealth from the nation these ingredients would reduce the amount of personal wealth available for the citizens to consume at the rate they had become accustom too. In order to continue to consume, they would start to borrow to keep pace. The American socialist both assisted and encouraged their citizens to borrow for consumption through the use of expanding the credit. They did this by manipulating both the interest rates which they controlled and by regulating the institutions that lent the citizens money (the banks). While the citizens lost portions of their wealth to government taxes, government borrowing and their purchasing power to the inflation of the currency, they became more and more inclined to go into personal debt in order to maintain their lifestyles. The American socialist superbly incorporated an atmosphere that would make its citizens believe that overtime the reason they had trouble maintaining their lifestyle was because they were either living beyond their means or simply not working hard enough. When manipulated correctly, the citizens will never realize that it is you, (through the use of these ingredients), who is fully responsible for reducing their means in the first place.

Once you steal your nation's available wealth, you must create an environment for them to borrow in order to keep your plan moving forward. Consumption is the key. Once the accumulated wealth is out of their hands and into yours, the economy will slow down, stop, and start to go into a depression. However, if you can get them to start borrowing to consume, they will start going into debt paying for it with the possible wealth from their future labor. This will allow you to steal from them today what you would have otherwise had to wait years to get your hands on. Reversing the concept from that of *savings* to that of *debt* to consume is imperative to the success of your long term plan.

Spend Their Money to Maximize Your Profits

"When the people find that they can vote themselves money, that will herald the end of the republic." -Benjamin Franklin

The way you spend your citizen's money is essential to giving you the ability to both steal it as well as allow your government to gain full control of the nation. There are two simplistic ways to accomplish this.

Step one: Allow your politicians to vote on how to spend your citizens money. Give members of your government the ability to pass legislation that will allow them to give your citizens money to their own special interest groups. You should create a practice of attaching these spending bills to other laws they are passing, burying the majority of the spending from the public eye. You can create a level of competition between your politicians in which they will work in unison to spend your citizen's money. For example, if one group of politicians wants to give away money to a particular group of their supporters but other politicians don't agree, swapping favors is the best way to overcome that. Encourage your politicians to work with each other and compromise their principles in the interest of getting what they want. Granting favor-for-favor in return should be encouraged. This will prompt your politicians to vote on spending bills that they don't agree with in order to persuade other politicians to vote for spending bills that they want to pass for their special interest groups.

Step two: Allow your politicians to set aside huge packages of money for your current administration to spend as they wish. This will cut the time it takes to spend huge sums of your citizen's money. For example, if your administration feels like it is going to take 900 billion dollars to "stimulate" your economy to keep your plan going, it may take too much time to pass enough spending bills in order to get that kind of money out into your economy to keep it afloat. If you are getting close to your depression, time may be of the essence. You can shorten the time it takes to dump huge portions of cash into your economy by convincing your politicians into passing very large "stimulus spending" bills. This way they can simply vote on a substantial dollar amount and grant your administration a huge portion of your citizen's wealth to spend the way they see fit. It is a way of cutting through all of the red-tape and it will allow you to burn through a large portion of your citizen's wealth in a very short period of time.

Of course, your entitlement spending (programs created that make your citizens dependent on you) will help you out tremendously when it comes to spending huge sums of your citizen's wealth. These programs will take great swaths of your nation's wealth annually and you are guaranteed that these programs will grow over time. While spending sounds like lots of fun, you will have to work at it. Most of your citizens can't even imagine spending a million dollars, so when it comes to spending billions and trillions it will take a level of talent. It can become a full time job just looking for programs and projects to waste your citizen's wealth on, in order to continue to spend at the rate that will be needed to keep both your economy and your opportunities going until your depression takes place.

In order to take over full control of your nation and keep it, you will want your government to eventually own the banks, land (both public and private), industry, labor and all of the natural resources. You can easily take ownership of all of these simply by following this recipe and using these ingredients.

First, you must gain a sound understanding of what constitutes ownership. For example, say someone purchases a television set but someone else has the right to tell them where they can put the T.V. in their home, when they can turn it on, and what programs they can view. Who actually owns the T.V.? Now I know this seems far-fetched, but the greatest depression creators have used this time tested method over and over again to gain *control* or *ownership* of their nations.

Regulate Regulate Regulate

Like a conductor of an orchestra, regulations will allow you to make your economy play exactly as you wish. Regulations are necessary to hide the evil effects of *inflation*. They will keep your citizens both unaware while at the same time creating the environment in which they will gladly trade their liberties for the false security of Government. Regulations are vital to your success. You must set up your government in a manner in which it can impose regulation after regulation upon your citizens. This is not only a great way to control your citizen's behavior and reduce their awareness, but it is necessary to hide the effects of your ingredient *inflation* as it does its dirty work. Like I mentioned before and will continue to touch on throughout this lesson, "***never, ever let a good crisis go to waste***". Remember, crises are your friend and ally. If a good crisis doesn't present itself in order to persuade your citizens into accepting the things you want to either change or control, then by all means create one.

The *Golden Rule* to implementing volumes of regulations is that you have to make your citizens believe that it is in both theirs and their countries best interest. The right *crisis* will almost always allow you to present the deception necessary to gain their agreement and increase an untold number of regulations upon them. If you want to regulate your banks, create a banking crisis which will allow you to impress upon your subjects that banking regulations are needed to prevent a crisis. *Inflation* will create havoc in your economy. It will force prices to go up on virtually everything that your citizens need to survive. This will allow you to create lots of rules and regulations all with the intent of controlling the effects of inflation while you grow your government. You will be able to regulate every major aspect of your economy from manufacturing, farming, health services, education and even the natural resources of your nation.

Regulations are a great way of hiding the effects of inflation when either passing laws lack political will, or the process just seems to take too much time. Regulations can be imposed simply by a department head in your government, when controlling either a section of the economy or a part of the population is desired. For example, the American socialists have many departments and agencies like the Environmental Protection Agency, the Department of Education, Commodity Credit Corporation, Commodity Futures Trading Commission, Drug Enforcement Administration, Employee and Training Administration, Equal Employment Opportunity Commission, Farm Credit Administration, Federal Energy Regulatory Commission, Food and Drug Administration, Federal Trade Commission, Federal Aviation Administration and the list goes on and on and on.... Each agency, possessing the right to impose restrictions and regulations to enforce the desired intent of the department itself on the people of the nation.

Regulations will allow you to pick winners and losers in your economy. For example, if you want to protect or even advance particular companies profit margins, you can implement regulations to keep other companies from competing with them. Let's say for example that there is a company that makes nice profits by manufacturing a drug that helps to treat cancer patients. Maybe you or some of your supporters have money invested in this company and you want to protect its profits. You can prevent other entrepreneurs and companies from competing with this company by simply using regulations. One idea would be to have an agency set up in your government that oversees both the research and manufacturing in the medical industry. Give this agency the ability to levy regulations and they can at will impose rules and guidelines making it impossible for other companies to compete or bring to market alternative solutions or treatments. Through regulations you may even be able to prevent cures for certain illness like cancer allowing the companies that you and your cohorts are vested in to continue to make profits from treatments that mask the illness vs. curing it. Regulations will allow you to both control and maximize profits for a few at the expense of the many.

REGULATE YOUR BANKING SYSTEM

Creating a National Banking System is just the first step in controlling how you allow your citizens to obtain capital for either consumption (consumer debt) or production (private corporate/business debt). Through the use of regulating your banking system, you will have the ability to own virtually all the private real estate when your citizens obtain a mortgage in order to make their purchase. You will be able to control the amount of capital available to the citizens that either have, want to start, or expand their own business. Regulations will allow you to pick and choose how many of your citizens are able to purchase their own home. You will achieve this by creating or restricting the available credit and controlling credit requirements.

Through the use of regulations, your government will be able to claim ownership of all the homes that have a mortgage when the people can no longer afford their payments. The beauty of this is that it doesn't even have to be a government backed loan. The regulations that you can impose on your banking system will make all mortgages guaranteed by your government. Whether it's a conventional loan (a standard type mortgage with a bank) or a government guaranteed loan like FHA, VA, or Rural Development (the government guarantee's the loan if it goes into default), your government will want to ensure through laws and regulations that they will be able to lay claim to all of their citizen's property when a mortgage goes into default. By the very nature of the depression you will create, you can insure that most mortgage holders will go into default. Of course, there are going to be a lot of older people as you approach your depression that will have already gained ownership of their homes and no longer have a mortgage. To correct this, you can start programs like the American socialist did. Your ingredient, inflation, will continue to erode your nation's ability to survive. So, in order to entice the older people who are on fixed incomes and have either paid off their mortgages or are close to paying them off, promoting *reverse mortgages* (the bank makes payments to the original home owner to help supplement their income as if they are purchasing the home back from you) will allow you to steal even their homes when your depression ensues. It will help to keep a number of homes from being passed down to the next generation and give your government more of the citizen's personal property that you can use to control them. Obtaining ownership of your nation's resources will allow you to reward your loyal followers by granting those that support you with bits and pieces of these resources. It will also give you the means to control your population since they will have to look to you for their means of survival.

Once again, you should follow the road map to total government land ownership put in place by the creators of American socialism. The genius of the American plan was to use the guise of insurance as the means to obtain that country's real estate. The creation of the FDIC (Federal Depositors Insurance Corporation) put in place during the Franklin Delano Roosevelt administration, coupled with the FED (Federal Reserve) instituted by Woodrow Wilson, would overtime give their government the means to take control of the nation's banks and all their assets. This also allowed them to set up laws that would allow them to take control of the assets of any "member" bank that fails. You only need to understand here that once one or any number of the member banks fails, the government could either bail those banks out using its citizen's money or simply seize control of the failed banks assets. The choice for their government would simply be based on if they were still laying the groundwork for their depression, or if their depression was now underway. Pre-depression, the bailout option would serve their purpose best in that it would accelerate the number of institutions indebted to them. Today, US banks own a greater share of residential housing net worth than all individual Americans put together. They can, by law, once their Great Depression gets underway, simply seize those assets and hold them for their government. This will assist them in controlling their citizens throughout their depression and leave them in full control of their nation even beyond their Great Depression. Philosophers tend to call this form of governing communism, but you will want to keep that quiet, especially in a nation in which the people still assume they are free. At least keep it quiet until you allow your depression to occur.

REGULATE THE PRIVATE SECTOR

Regulations will allow you to take ownership of the private business sector. The last thing you want to do is go sparingly on the amount of regulations that you impose on your citizens. You

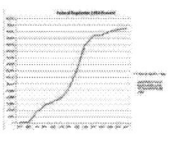

Federal Regulations

must do everything possible to strike a balance between allowing them to create enough wealth for you to steal, while at the same time keeping a heavy hand of control on how you allow them to operate. Inflation all by itself will create literally thousands of crises that will allow you to impose untold numbers of regulations on your citizens. If you manipulate it just right, you will actually create an environment in which a good portion of your citizens will beg you to regulate their lives in what they believe will be in their best interest.

You will want to regulate just about everything the private sector does in order to gain full control. You should regulate their labor by controlling the hours they can work and conditions they can work in. You will want to regulate their health care benefits, how much they have to pay you for employing people and how much they and their employees are allowed to pay for their future retirements. You will want to control how much they will need to pay for the freedom to own a business, what types of permits they will need and how much they will have to pay you for them. You will want to impose regulations and fees for giving them permission to export their products to other countries and yet more regulations and fees for allowing them to import from other countries. You will want to regulate through subsidizing the types of food your farmers can grow and you will want to pay farmers to not grow certain foods at all. You will want to incorporate price controls on certain commodities to both hide the effects of your inflation and to create environments that allow you to take advantage of the price swings you create while controlling these areas of the economy.

As you grow your government, regulations can be imposed by the many government agencies you create. You can impose regulations through your associates and accomplices holding government positions. You can also regulate by using taxes and imposing fees on particular areas of your economy. You should start up huge government bureaucracies using your citizen's money to cover the cost of controlling them. You must impose as many government regulations on your citizens as possible. Regulations will not only give you control and ownership over every facet of your citizen's lives, it will also serve to lessen the overall level of learning that would normally occur through an evolving citizenry. As you regulate business, industry, and your citizens, you will take away the incentive for people to make their own decisions. Regulations effectively reduce the necessity for your citizens to think for themselves or take personal responsibility in many areas of their lives. In essence, you will begin to do their thinking for them. This will allow you years of opportunity to steal their wealth. Remember, regulation gives you ownership without actually having to hold title. As long as you can control how your citizens are allowed to conduct their business and live their lives, you own them.

Through the use of both regulations and taxation, you can take over control of the natural resources of your nation. For example, if you want to stop a particular resource from being used, you can simply impose a heavy tax on that resource to diminish the consumption which will reduce the production. Conversely, if you want to promote growth in a particular area of your economy that will benefit you, simply subsidize it using your taxpaying citizens money and that area will grow for as long as you throw money at it. This is an effective way to grow your personal wealth. Simply invest your own capital in these areas that you are going to subsidize ahead of time and then once you stimulate using the tax payer's money, the value of your personal investment will increase. Remove or sell your investments before the stimulus wears off in order to maximize your profits.

If you want to encourage imports or exports of products, regulation and taxation are guaranteed ways to control the outcome. Regulations will be a handy tool in your toolbox to control economic outcomes. They will help you to both hide the effects of inflation and allow you to force your nation's economy to operate exactly as you wish.

Regulations will help you to grow your government, giving you the opportunity to start literally hundreds of *regulatory agencies*. You can assign your cohorts to head these agencies, allowing you to return favors to them. This will allow you to secure loyal followers allowing them both power and a piece of your citizens wealth. As you get closer to your Great Depression you must realize that chaos will ensue amongst your citizens. It will be important that you have all your players in the right areas of your government in order to take full control of the citizens quickly, or your government might risk falling apart.

Maximize Your Personal Profits

Creating a National Banking System is just the first step in controlling how you allow your citizens to obtain capital for either consumption (consumer debt) or production (private corporate/business debt). Through the use of regulating your banking system, you will have the ability to own virtually all the private real estate when your citizens obtain a mortgage in order to make their purchase. You will be able to control the amount of capital available to the citizens that either have, want to start, or expand their own business. Regulations will allow you to pick and choose how many of your citizens are able to purchase their own home. You will achieve this by creating or restricting the available credit and controlling credit requirements.

Through the use of regulations, your government will be able to claim ownership of all the homes that have a mortgage when the people can no longer afford their payments. The beauty of this is that it doesn't even have to be a government backed loan. The regulations that you can impose on your banking system will make all mortgages guaranteed by your government. Whether it's a conventional loan (a standard type mortgage with a bank) or a government guaranteed loan like FHA, VA, or Rural Development (the government guarantee's the loan if it goes into default), your government will want to ensure through laws and regulations that they will be able to lay claim to all of their citizen's property when a mortgage goes into default. By the very nature of the depression you will create, you can insure that most mortgage holders will go into default. Of course, there are going to be a lot of older people as you approach your depression that will have already gained ownership of their homes and no longer have a mortgage. To correct this, you can start programs like the American socialist did. Your ingredient, inflation, will continue to erode your nation's ability to survive. So, in order to entice the older people who are on fixed incomes and have either paid off their mortgages or are close to paying them off, promoting *reverse mortgages* (the bank makes payments to the original home owner to help supplement their income as if they are purchasing the home back from you) will allow you to steal even their homes when your depression ensues. It will help to keep a number of homes from being passed down to the next generation and give your government more of the citizen's personal property that you can use to control them. Obtaining ownership of your nation's resources will allow you to reward your loyal followers by granting those that support you with bits and pieces of these resources. It will also give you the means to control your population since they will have to look to you for their means of survival.

While Capitalism would by its very nature enforce the concept that those who hold public office are in fact public servants, Socialism will allow you to make public office a business and a very big business indeed. This will create an entire class of people who will aspire to hold office with the intent of becoming both rich and secure at the expense of their nation. They will be called the Government class.

Maximizing your own personal profits and that of your associates is probably the easiest part of the plan while creating your national depression. First, by understanding that your government has three and only three ways to generate its income; taxing, borrowing and inflating and that all three of these methods will create a depression. Second, having the insight that the way you *spend* that money can and will control your nation's economy. Understanding those two things will make it very easy to incorporate methods to destroy the wealth of your nation and in the process create great opportunities for both yourself and your accomplices. You don't have to look too far to find literally thousands of examples of people just like yourself that entered public office with little to no personal fortune, yet over a short period of time amassed huge sums of money for themselves. Likewise, there are hundreds of examples in which people that already have huge fortunes either entered public office or paid to assist others to gain public office who multiplied many times their original treasures. Socialism will allow you to create an environment in which men will spend millions to secure a job that pays the recipient only a fraction of what it cost to procure it.

If you implement your ingredients to create your national depression as I have outlined, you will successfully change the entire concept of what public office actually is in your nation. Here again, capitalism is your enemy. You must destroy capitalism if it exists at the onset of your plan and you must always guard against any form of capitalism from springing up along the way. Just like reversing the laws of economics, socialism will allow you to reverse the concept of public office from that of public servant to that of *serving up the public*. While capitalism would by its very nature enforce the concept that those who hold public office are in fact public servants.

There are several ways that you can increase your power and gain huge profits for yourself and your associates while you destroy the wealth of your nation.

- Make your personal investments based on the areas of the economy that your government is stimulating. You can accomplish this through either the use of the stock market, direct investment into private companies themselves, personal ownership of your own companies or ideally a combination of all three.
- Encourage and accept kick-backs: Encourage businesses and organizations to make direct payments to you for passing either legislation or regulations that will benefit their companies or organizations. This is a great way to increase your personal wealth and when performed correctly can be done without the public ever becoming aware of it.
- Create *"bills"* that will allow you to hide all kinds of spending at the taxpayers' expense. Most bills you create are really *future payments* that your citizens will be responsible for paying by law. Once your future payments are signed into law, your citizens will be on the hook for the bills you and your associates create.
- Allow or create an atmosphere in which large sums of money can be donated to you in order to support your reelection. You will be able to pocket some of this money and it will create a large number of opportunities for you as you repay

these favors to your donors. As you spend your citizen's money in a manner that supports your donor's interests, you will also be free to make personal investments at the public's expense.

By now you should have a good understanding that it isn't necessary to actually put your hands into your government's treasury in order to seize your fortunes. Your hands just have to be the ones that direct the flow of money out of your nation's treasury. You simply need to create an environment whereby the means that your government generates revenue, coupled with the means by which it spends that revenue, will present the opportunities needed for you and your associates to usurp the wealth of your nations citizens. Using this recipe will create untold opportunities for you and members of your government to realize huge financial gains along the way. It will also allow you to create a government structure that you can use to protect both you and your cohorts once the public becomes aware of the level of your deception.

5

The End Game

All good things must come to an end.

It's one thing to understand how to create a national depression so that you can create huge profits at the expense of your citizens, but it is another to be able to know when the end is near or when your Great Depression will take root and collapse your nations economy. As you can see, the road to your depression is where the real opportunities lie, but the depression itself can be a real game changer depending on what type of depression you allow to occur.

There are two types of economic depressions, each having its own very different outcome. It will be totally up to you depending on your goals as to the type of Great Depression you will want to create. If you followed the road map laid out here, deciding upon and promoting one of the two types of depressions is very simple.

Assessing Your Goals

This part is rather simple. Ask yourself if you've accumulated enough wealth on the road to your depression for you and your followers? Are you willing to stop your plan, or do you require yet more wealth and power? The answer to this question will determine the type of depression you will want to promote.

If you've gained enough personal wealth and are willing to allow your depression to take place in a manner that could allow your nation's economy to return to the control of the people (capitalism), you can promote a *deflationary* depression. This will provide an outside chance that the citizens could regain their freedoms and liberties and control their own wealth once again.

On the other hand, if your goal is to maintain control over the people by keeping your citizens under economic bondage, then you will want to create a *hyper-inflationary* depression. This will allow you to transform your nation from socialism to communism, the next form of government on the evolutionary chain. Either way, it is pretty much within your government's power to orchestrate either one.

Deflation vs. Hyperinflation

If you followed this road map to creating a national depression, you *should* have the ability to pick and choose which depression you will allow to occur. I say should, because there could come a point on your road to creating your national depression that if you inflate both your currency and credit too much, your depression will automatically become a *hyper-inflationary* depression.

A deflationary depression is one in which an economy collapses after it has been overextended for a period of time. It allows the economy to go through a period of correction. Throughout this period, there is a time of great suffrage amongst the people of the nation until the depression bottoms out and the economy begins to recover. Once a deflationary depression hits its bottom, the economy, if no longer hampered or interfered with by a government, can spring back allowing the citizens of its nation to prosper once again.

*****Caution***** if you allow a deflationary depression to occur, you risk the chance that the citizens of your nation will once again find *freedom* and return to *capitalism* as their economic philosophy. This will prevent you from usurping further wealth at the expense of the citizens. Only allow this type of depression to occur if you and your government no longer have the need or desire to continue to steal that nations wealth. That is not to say that once the nation recovers you or another group of thieves won't be able to go back in and start the entire process over. You do risk the chance that the citizens will start to accumulate knowledge through evolution once again, and will put into place laws forever preventing government intervention into their lives. However, even if they do that, the best laid constitutions can be successfully circumvented by using this recipe for creating depressions. As long as the people are willing to drop their guard and allow a group of thieves to use any crisis in order to exchange their liberties for the promise of government security, their nation will always be at risk. The bottom line here is that a deflationary depression will allow for the citizens who still have some capital left to assist their nation in recovering from what you did to them, whereas a hyper-inflationary depression will not.

A *Hyper-Inflationary Depression* is one in which your government inflates both the currency and the available credit you require your citizens to use until your mandated currency becomes absolutely worthless. This type of depression totally eliminates the wealth of all of its citizens, even those who have accumulated it and hold it in either your currency or through other means such as investments, stocks, bonds, T-bills, government securities, savings accounts, pensions etc. Suddenly, even those individuals who thought they had accumulated wealth over the years, find themselves left with absolutely nothing.

This is the type of depression you will want to pursue if your goal is to ultimately enslave the citizens of your nation permanently for both yourself and your government. A hyper-inflationary depression will ensure an extreme level of chaos throughout your nation as it occurs. It leaves literally no one left with the ability to help get the nation out of the depression. If you implemented all the ingredients in order to create a national depression correctly, the vast majority of your population will be very ill prepared when your hyper-inflationary depression takes place.

While the road to a hyper-inflationary depression can be lengthy, the realization that the currency has become valueless can take hours or mere moments. It is highly possible once you reach this point that the vast majority of your population will have less than a one week supply of food, limited drinking water, and no money of any value. They will know few, if any, individuals that have enough resources to take care of themselves let alone take care of others. As the house of cards falls, within hours there will be literally millions of people rushing to grocery stores to purchase what they can with the worthless dollars they possess. It will take no time at all to empty the shelves. Within the first hours of your hyper-inflationary depression, riots in densely populated cities will begin to emerge. It won't take long for those populations to realize that the money they possess has become worthless paper. Just like the hyperinflation that took place in Germany less than one short century ago, burning that money to keep warm will be its most valuable use.

Commerce will cease to exist. Banks, businesses, government agencies, public services, corporations large and small will all instantly lose the ability to pay their employees. Farmers will not allow their goods to go to market in exchange for worthless dollars and even if they wanted to, there would be no trucks or truck drivers that will transport goods and services for free. Oil companies will no longer sell gas for worthless dollars. Manufacturers, caners, fisherman, water, gas and oil companies, convenience stores, grocers, restaurants, doctors offices, hospitals, pharmaceutical companies, schools, cable T.V., radio, satellite services, old-folks homes, mental institutions, the prison systems, police, fireman, the courts, city, state and federal agencies will all stop functioning. The nation will instantly go from a currency system to that of a barter system exactly like several socialist nations have experienced throughout history. Examples of this are Germany in 1922, Hungary in 1945, Chile in 1971, Argentina in 1975, Peru in 1988, Angola in 1991, Yugoslavia in 1992, Belarus in 1994 and Zimbabwe in 2000. All nations that hyper-inflated their currency and in the process left their people devastated. These nations left their citizens to bartering while their governments frantically attempted to replace their inflated currency with yet another fiat currency in their pursuit to maintain control.

If hyperinflation is the depression you choose for your nation, you will need to take some measures to control the ensuing chaos that is certain to occur amongst your population.

Disarm Your Nation

If you intend to maintain control of your nation by forcing a hyperinflation of your currency, there are some steps that you must take in order to secure yourself and your government. First and foremost, ***if the citizens of your nation have the right to bear arms, you must disarm them prior to the onset of your hyper-inflationary depression.*** An armed nation in a hyper-inflationary depression is a grave danger to both you and your controlling government. A hyper-inflationary depression will wake a population from their slumber, and the anger of your nation will be no less than that of awakening a grizzly bear from its hibernation with a hot poker. You must do everything within your power using any means necessary to disarm your nation. Once again, ***never let a good crisis go to waste.*** If one doesn't present itself, create one! Keep an eye on events that happen in your nation and use any mention of gun violence against innocent people as the catalyst to begin convincing your citizens that you can better protect them if guns are banned. Examples of violence against children will be your best weapon to convincing the masses that disarming them will be in the nations best interest. Even if statistics clearly show the opposite to be true, if you have reached this point in your depression, and you are ready to hyper-inflate the money supply, then you have without a doubt had great success at stunting both common sense and logic amongst your citizens. You should at this point have a majority of people that will go along with just about anything you put in front of them, and they will happily allow your government to secure them for their own good.

Next, on the road to your hyper-inflationary depression, amass great military strength. **Creating a very large formidable military,** will allow you to use your citizens wealth to eventually control them. Over the years, as you implement your plan to steal your nations wealth, you can use huge sums of your citizens money to invest in your military. This will create tremendous opportunities to divert substantial portions of their wealth to different corporations increasing you and your cohorts prospects to build your personal fortunes. Fear is a tremendous motivator. If you can manipulate your citizens into thinking a large military is needed to prevent foreign aggression against them, you can **turn that fear into permission** allowing you to achieve this goal. It would be prudent as well, to create internal law enforcement agencies on a national scale. If presented correctly, you will be able to convince your citizens that a large organization, designed to protect them within their own boarders, is necessary for their safety and security. This will allow you to move military equipment to such an organization. It will be important that you plan for your citizens uprising against you when they come to understand that you have destroyed their currency and ruined their way of life. One thing you should learn and always remember no government can survive without the support of its people. You must be prepared to put down any uprising or any form of protest from your population by any means necessary. By having a formidable internal security force that is well armed, you will be able to move quickly against any part of your population that has held on to any belief that freedom is a better option than what you are now offering.

CREATE A STRONG MILITARY

A strong, large military will be of utmost importance to prevent your citizens and your nation from completely falling apart. You can impose curfews keeping people off the streets during hours of darkness in an attempt to stave off massive theft and violence that the people will most likely inflict upon each other in their attempts to survive. *Martial law* should be an option in attempts to keep the peace. At the same time, by Executive order, you can use your military force if necessary to compel your citizens to go to work and continue their jobs without the benefit of being paid for their labor (*Communism*). Since inflation will have rendered extinct the concept of profit as the motivator for labor, you will have to replace it with a new concept, **fear**. Fear is a tremendous motivator and one that by now you should be able to manipulate. Fear of hunger, fear of starvation, fear for one's life and that of their families, fear of their neighbors and, if need be, fear of your government will be necessary to get your citizens to produce for their very survival and the survival of your government.

You will most likely want to position members of your military in parts of the country that are far from their homes and preferably in areas that are predominantly populated by opposing political beliefs than their own. There is great risk in positioning your soldiers close to their homes because they may be reluctant to carry out orders against their friends and families. Equally, if you've done an adequate job of dividing your nation politically, stationing them in regions of opposite political affiliation will create an atmosphere of conflict which will aid you in getting them to follow out extreme orders against the population. If you play your cards right, your citizens will not even know what hit them. Just like today, most Americans are unaware that they are living under a socialist economy; they will never know that they have become a *communist* nation. Most will continue to blame *capitalism*, the only thing that could have saved them as the culprit for their reduced standard of living and loss of liberty.

6

SAVING A NATION

Realizing that the deception taking place in America has been going on for exactly one hundred years now will help us understand that we are faced with generations born into a culture fraught with deception and thievery. Today, the occupants of this once great nation cannot by-and-large be held responsible for their lack of knowledge when it comes to the government or the people that have continued to take advantage of the ground work laid in the beginning of the twentieth century. Not only have they been born into it, but all of their parents and even most of their grandparents were born into this tainted environment. While there are many Americans who have been able to see through the fog, they are a very small number. The vast majority of Americans are unaware, simply because they were born into this environment. The majority of Americans when asked what *inflation* is cannot even begin to explain it. They have never lived through a severe depression, nor do they have an understanding of what the nation was like prior to *inflation.* They have a tendency to believe that a national economic meltdown and the chaos that occurs during one simply won't occur. Sadly, this will leave well over ninety percent of the population absolutely unprepared. Once they are jolted out of this normalcy bias it will be way too late for them to have any control over their lives.

The problem with economists is that they write for other economists. Philosophers write for philosophers and politicians, when they aren't stealing, write for other politicians. Very few either write, or for that matter even talk in a manner that the vast majority of the population can understand. Today, we have literally millions of people that go to the poles and cast a vote without possessing a fraction of understanding as to how those they elect will affect their lives.

German economist and philosopher Karl Marx believed that there would be a natural progression from Capitalism to Socialism and then to Communism throughout the world. In the end, he surmised that the world would live at peace in a "Communist Utopia". In my opinion, Karl Marx had a level of contempt for Capitalism, and while I believe that the majority of his philosophies have been fraught with inconsistencies since their writing, history has shown us that nations operating under both socialism and communism simply do not sustain themselves. An area in which I believe Marx was partially right was that nations would change from capitalism to socialism to communism. However I disagree with Marx's opinion that he called it a natural progression, whereas I would call it a regression. I believe Marx to be dead wrong in his belief that this would deliver *Utopian* results. History has clearly documented that both socialism and communism uniquely dis-incentivizes the people of the nation when these philosophies are put into practice. No different than what has occurred in the United States over the last one hundred years. Unfortunately, people lose the incentive to work when what they are making comes close to or equals what the government is willing to give them to survive. The nonproductive sector will always continue to grow as the productive sector is pillaged, shrinking as it succumbs to the nonproductive sector. Wealth is reduced and debt is increased until it can no longer be sustained. Neither Socialism nor Communism has EVER sustained or increased the standard of living of its people.

A common thread amongst philosophers that tout socialism and communism is their lack of trust in man. They tend to believe that *Men* if left unattended to their *freewill* will somehow become a detriment to society as a whole. They put their trust in governing bodies with the thought that a government has a better capacity to guide and steer a people to peace and prosperity, yet history supports the opposite to be true. In my opinion, what philosophers like Marx and Lenin did not consider was that the governments they would rather trust would indeed be run by men, and that their very skepticism of what free men might do to the collective would be compounded by their ability to control governments of nations.

Countries like Communist China and Soviet Russia are shining examples of nations that embraced both of those philosophies which delivered to their nations some of the lowest standards of living among industrialized nations. It wasn't until both China and Russia started to open up free markets and grant some personal liberties, that their people have finally started to produce and create wealth. With the Chinese Economic Reform starting in 1978 and continuing up through the 1980s, we can see how moving from communism and socialism towards some form of capitalism in these nations has increased the standard of living for their people. With the fall of the Berlin wall and the breakup of the Union of Soviets Socialists Republics, we have witnessed many of the former satellite nations like Poland and Bulgaria move away from central planning to a more free market environment which has increased the standard of living for the peoples of these nations. Conversely, we can see how changing from capitalism to socialism while on the road to communism in the United States of America has reversed the trend from creating wealth to creating debt which has ultimately reduced the standard of living for our people.

The Measure of Our Freedom

While money may not be everything, it is an accurate measure of our economic freedom. An acquaintance of mine after reading one of my articles on inflation asked me how I could tie freedom to inflation. His

Measure of Money

opinion was that he hadn't really seen any proof that the government is taking away any of our freedoms and that he saw nothing to suggest that we would end up a less free nation due to our governments spending or inflation. I cherish questions like this, because not only do they come from people engaged in our process who have a genuine concern, but it allows for a debate to take place around the greatest issue we face as a nation today.

So, while money may not be everything, as the rate of inflation increases, our personal freedoms decrease. If you agree that math is a true science and you have any understanding of the impact that inflation has on your money, than you have to agree that over the years the value of your dollars have diminished consistently taking more dollars to purchase the same goods and services today than it took yesterday.

How Does Money Measure Our Freedom?

The truth is so very simple. Whether you don't have enough money to do the things that you want to do for your family, or the money that you do have has become worth less (taking more dollars to purchase the same amount of goods and services you have purchased in the past). As a result, you become less free to do the things you want to do.

For example, your money measures if you are free to own a home, buy a car, take a vacation, put the appropriate amount of food on the table for you family, send your kids to college, buy clothing, go to a movie, put your kids in extra-curricular activities, insure your health, own a TV, get service to your TV, own a phone, have a savings account, get a tank of gas, heat or air condition your home and the list goes on and on. Money, either having a lot or too little, impacts virtually everything that you do or want to do in your life. Money and money alone is the only indicator that can be used to determine if you are *free* to do any of these things.

Look at our class structure. Those in the middle class enjoy a greater amount of freedom than those impoverished or dependent on the government. We have more power to purchase homes, cars, adequate health-care or in general more comforts for our families than the class below us. At the same time, those in the upper middle class and on up into the upper class enjoy greater freedoms than those in the middle or lower segments of the middle class. Is this due to a different set of rules for those classes? No, it is simply the measurement of money held on average in these separate classes. No matter the class, inflation erodes the level of freedom equally for all.

It cannot be contested that the rate of inflation or the erosion of the dollar has far outpaced the rate of increases in our incomes. This disparity has, year after year, been responsible for reducing what we can afford today in comparison to the past. Inflation by its nature escalates at an ever increasing pace, and eventually towards the end of a hyper-inflationary cycle, incomes will begin to diminish as businesses take extreme measures to protect their profits from the effects of inflation.

Once you understand how money measures your freedom, it becomes easier to understand that our freedom is reduced as the rate of inflation increases. Every single one of our elected officials over the years have either known this and used this to usurp power for themselves and others around them, or are so clearly unaware of reality that they should be removed from office. Any one of our elected officials who do not place stopping inflation at the very top of their agenda i.e. reducing and eliminating the debt, stop the out of control government spending, pay down the national debt, balance the budget, eliminate the FED and forever ban inflating our currency, in my opinion is simply not worth a vote.

The Greatest Government Deception in World History

"The high office of the President has been used to formant a plot to destroy the American's freedom and before I leave office I must inform the Citizen of his plight."

PRESIDENT JOHN F. KENNEDY (In a speech made at Columbia University on November 12th, 1963, 10 days before he was murdered)

Magic is an act of deception performed for entertainment purposes. This art is one of trickery— using deception with the intent of making the onlookers believe that an impossible outcome has been achieved. Magic challenges our perception for a moment in time. While entertaining, the majority of the adult audience accepts that magic is an act of deception. Once the method of the act is revealed, the magic, magically disappears.

As a child in America growing up in the 60's and 70's, I grew up with the understanding that the United States was one of the few nations on earth in which people were free. We were taught in our schools that people who lived in countries like China and the Soviet Union lived under the thumb of their governments. These governments controlled what people were allowed to see, hear, read and write about. We all understood that freedom was kept from these people so that their governments could control them. There was a general feeling during that era that if these people could just know and understand us for who we were, if their government would just allow freedom like we had, then those people kept ignorant about us Americans would no longer hate us for being free. Little did we know or even consider back then that our very own government, the government that we pledged our allegiance to, was covering up the largest deception ever perpetrated on a nation's people.

Through the use of inflation as the method of deception, the Federal Reserve (privately owned banks) in conjunction with many members of the government of the United States of America has robbed, pick-pocketed, fleeced, stripped and raided the American citizens of their wealth. Inflation has destroyed our citizen's purchasing power and it has altered the moral fiber of our nation. This deception has run so deep and has been so thoroughly hidden it is indeed a mind blowing reality. Few either know or understand what has taken place. For the ones that do, trying to educate the ones that do not becomes a daunting task. Imagine trying to wake up a nation of people that has long been asleep, preferring their slumber over the realization of how this knowledge would impact their lives. Most prefer to hold on to the false sense of security hanging on to the belief that the government will always take care of them. That very concept and thought process alone, is so contrary to whom we once were, that this type of thinking is simply an American tragedy. Most find comfort in the magic act as if the magician can somehow change their fantasy to reality. They fancy the thought that the Magician can make their lives somehow mystically better as long as they continue to believe in the trickery.

Stealing a Nations Wealth

Stealing; 1: to take the property of another wrongfully and especially as a habitual or regular practice 2: to come or go secretly, unobtrusively, gradually, or unexpectedly

"The money powers prey upon the nation in times of peace and conspire against it in times of adversity. It is more depotic than a monarchy, more insolent than autocracy and more selfish than a bureaucracy. It denounces, as public enemies, all who question its methods or throw light upon its crimes. I have two great enemies, the Southern Army in front of me and the bankers in the rear. Of the two, the one at the rear is my greatest foe." - PRESIDENT ABRAHAM LINCOLN - 1866

Not unlike *taxation without representation*, the Federal Reserve in conjunction with many members past and present of the government of the United States of America has *stolen the wealth of its people without permission or legal right and without intending to return it*. While I understand that this is a very bold statement, you just might come to the exact same conclusion that I have come to over the last thirty years. Everyone who is alive today and living in the United States, whether wealthy or poor, surely sees that from month to month, year over year, that the cost of goods and services continues to rise. At the same time, for the vast majority of Americans, their income has not kept up with cost of living increases. Most believe this to be an effect of economic reality and therefore something we must just simply learn to live with. The truth of the matter is, this is both caused and created by the owners of the American banking system the "Federal Reserve" and the government. It is a method of stealing wealth from the public in order to continue to preserve the ruling government class.

Stripping Away Your Purchasing Power

Purchasing power refers to the amount of goods and services you can obtain based on the number of dollars you have to spend. For the vast majority of Americans, the dollars we have are limited from week to week and month to month. Any increase in the number of our dollars would be dependent on events such as a raise from our employer, a change in job, or in some cases money returned from investments. For the most part however, the majority of Americans live on a specific number of dollars throughout any given year with a possible minimum raise in income annually from our employers. The number of dollars we hold directly dictates the amount of goods and services we can obtain. Of course we can borrow more dollars if we have good credit, but still the borrowed money requires re-payment and in effect actually reduces your future purchasing power because it takes a portion of your annual income to pay for the money borrowed with *interest*.

The Federal Reserve in conjunction with the government of the United States of America has stripped you and every other member of our nation of its purchasing power over the last one hundred years. In fact, it has used inflation to rob you of the majority of your purchasing power from the early 1900s. Let's take a look at a smaller segment of time, say from 1965 to 2011, comparing both income and cost of living increases.

The median income of families according to the *Bureau of Census, Department of Commerce* in 1965 was $6,900. The national median income for 2011 was $50,054.00. I haven't seen the U.S. Census report for 2012 yet, but 2011 is close enough. This represents an increase of 625% over the last forty six years. Not bad huh? One would think and actually the government is banking on you thinking that a 625% increase in the average income is absolutely wonderful. Most Americans that I talk to will undoubtedly retort when we talk about the cost of living, that all things are equal because our wages are considerably higher today than they were in years gone by. My immediate response to that opinion, is that if all things are equal, why inflate the currency? Let's examine just how true that theory is;

Product 1965 avg. prices 2012 avg. Prices % of increase

✻ *Bread .21 cents $3.19 1419% increase*

✻ *Candy bar .05 cents $1.00 1900% increase*

✻ *Gallon Milk .99 cents $4.25 347% increase*

✻ *Gallon Gas .27 cents $3.29 1118% increase*

✻ *New Car $2,650.00 $30,000 1032% increase*

✻ *New home $14,500.00 $225,000.00 1451% increase*

These are just a few examples, but I assure you that this scenario is played out in virtually everything you purchase or have purchased over the years, and the kicker is, it is about to get much, much worse.

If we just take these few items and average out the percent of increase, it totals 1044% during this time period. Now bump that up against the percent of wage increase from the same time and you will see that at today's numbers, your purchasing power has decreased exactly forty percent from what it was just fifty years ago. The reality of it is forty percent of your income has been stolen by the Federal Reserve and members of our government through the use of inflation just since 1965, and the numbers look much worse if you go all the way back to 1913. Just stop reading for a moment and close your eyes and imagine how your life would be if you could have purchased almost twice as much as you can today on your current income. Imagine over your lifetime, what life would be like if you could have purchased or saved nearly twice as much as what you currently have over the last fifty, forty, thirty, twenty or even the past five years. Imagine what the nation might look like if its entire citizenry had maintained their purchasing power. How many more things could have been consumed or produced? How much more wealth vs. debt could have been created? Currently the *real* annual rate of inflation is estimated to be ten percent. At this rate, the American consumers purchasing power will be cut in half every seven years.

Since the 1960s, there has been a dramatic increase from single income to dual income households which is a direct effect of inflation. In the United States, households in which just the husband is the sole supporter has dropped to twenty one percent. Yet even with dual incomes, it seems as though Americans still have trouble keeping pace with the purchasing power that just a single income family had in the 1950s and 1960s.

For most of us that are old enough to remember, we grew up in households with a single income that was sufficient to support a household. Not only support the household, but support statistically much larger households at a higher standard of living than the smaller dual income households of today. Again; this is a direct result of the Federal Reserve and the US government reducing your wealth over many years through the use of inflation.

By Force or by Finance, Slavery is Slavery

All of us have seen plays or movies in which a government or ruler is either stealing its subject's wealth or simply enslaving the citizens for its own benefit. We cheer on the men who stand and fight against these *evil rulers*, yet when faced with the same reality in our own nation, we turn a blind eye. We hope that either a savior will come along and make things right, or somehow the very government that deceives and enslaves us will come to their senses. We would like to believe that the representatives we elect today will change direction and right the wrongs that officials before them have imposed on the people. Yet year after year, the American public continues to watch their savings dwindle and their lives become more difficult to afford. No matter the controlling party, the outcome remains the same. We have more national, corporate and personal debt, reduced purchasing power, and a greater struggle to survive. Whether by force or finance, slavery is slavery.

If you think about it, when a government controls or otherwise owns your labor, you are indeed a slave to that government. A government doesn't have to own your job or be your direct employer, it simply just has to control the money supply and dictate to its citizens how much that money supply is worth. The Federal Reserve both owns our money and dictates what that money is worth. Through the manipulation of inflation, the FED not only regulates how much money is available, but it is in total control of the value of it as well.

In order for the government to continue to expand and insure its existence for the many politicians and their cohorts, they tax us and borrow from us. They continue to attempt to raise our taxes and borrow more. When it becomes politically unfeasible to tax and borrow at a higher rate, they run up what is called a *deficit* (this is the difference between what they tax and spend). They then turn around and give the Federal Reserve (the private wealthy banker's) an equal amount of our citizens assets (government securities, Treasury bills), the FED then turns around and prints up an equal amount of currency and credits it to the US Treasury to pay the remainder of it's bills for that year. This is called *deficit spending*. It is the actual engine of inflation that is diminishing the value of all the currency we as citizens currently hold. It is the primary reason that prices go up and what you are able to afford goes down. It is a softer, more subtle act and one that by and large goes unnoticed by the general public.

For most, our concept of slavery is that of a ruler using whips, chains and invoking fear to exact labor and obedience from his subjects. We think of ancient times when the Egyptians enslaved a portion of their population for labor, or envision the Roman Empire were history records a similar slavery. Hitting closer to home, we might think of the enslavement of African Americans when our ancestors purchased and enslaved people as forced labor right here in America. Obviously, these are forms of forced slavery through viscous means. It is a type of slavery that is unlikely (I think) to be seen again here in America. Saying that, economic slavery is no less a type of slavery and is equally as evil. Take the slavery of the African American in this country. Americans like to think that slavery ended with the Emancipation Proclamation followed by the 13th Amendment in 1865, banning slavery in America. When you think about it, what the 13th amendment did was simply ban ownership of another human being. It did absolutely nothing to guarantee economic freedom or equality for African Americans. The black population remained in economic slavery for nearly one hundred years after their so called freedom was granted to them. They could not bank where they wanted to bank; they could not eat where they wanted to eat and were refused the same opportunity to make money or even hold the same type of jobs as whites. Their slavery through economics hit every aspect of their lives. From the places they could live to where their children could go to school, the binds of slavery were very much felt by the entire black population up to and through the Civil Rights movement of 1955 through 1968 and every bit of it through economic disparity.

The manipulation of the laws of economics via government intervention is a sure way to enslave an entire nation. Vladimir Lenin is said to have declared that *"the best way to destroy the capitalist system was to debauch the currency. By a continuing process of inflation, governments can confiscate, secretly and unobserved, an important part of the wealth of their citizens. By this method they not only confiscate, but they confiscate arbitrarily; and, while the process impoverishes many, it actually enriches some"*. He went on to say: "*There is no subtler, no surer means of overturning the existing basis of society than to debauch the currency. The process engages all the hidden forces of economic law on the side of destruction, and does it in a manner which not one man in a million is able to diagnose."*

This was acknowledged by John Maynard Keynes *(the father of our current economic practices)* whose economic philosophy the United States adopted during the Franklin Delano Roosevelt era.

While many will disagree with my take on economics and the current state of our once great Republic, there are many who see with clarity the exact same historical and economic calamities that are unfolding today in America. There are no grey areas here, after all, grey is just a combination of black and white dots that when separated become two very distinct colors. Americans are caught up in the fog that has been blanketed upon them by both their government, the Federal Reserve and the government controlled media. Today, Americans get caught up in the literally thousands of effects from *inflation* that their government and the media would have them focus on, never getting to the real issue or the real cause that has brought us to this point in history.

Looking forward, I wonder if the last four generations of Americans will be written about as the most deceived generation of people in the history of mankind. I believe that we will be remembered for what we are: a nation of socialist's who had no idea that we were socialist. It may well be written that we were a people of mass ignorance in a day and age of tremendous technology, in which the opportunity to gain knowledge was instead wasted on entertainment and self-indulgence.

"I fear the day when the technology overlaps with our humanity. The world will only have a generation of idiots." — Albert Einstein

7

THE IDIOCRACY OF OUR DEMOCRACY

I am a true believer in democracy. I believe in personal freedom, limited government and the idea that a government should be *for the people and by the people.* Saying that, I have great difficulty believing in or supporting the form of democracy that has stripped the wealth of our once great nation. Our form of democracy has deteriorated the fiber of the American family. It has destroyed the hopes and dreams of future American generations and incinerated the very core of what truly was a shining hope for all of mankind. However, I do believe that our Republic, governed under a form of democracy is still the best approach. I believe that it is the only form of government that could possibly allow *Man* the ability to live as God intended: *free.* I still believe that democracy allows for a nation to be prosperous and to grow beyond any nation governed by other philosophies. At the same time, I also understand without any reservation, that the form of democracy that our Republic has allowed to take over has failed miserably. The real question however is, did democracy fail "*We the people,*" or did "*We the people,*" fail our democracy?

Failing Our Democracy

We literally turned the keys of our kingdom willingly over to those who seek only to serve themselves.

There is no question in my mind that we the people have failed our democracy. Over the last one hundred years we have twisted, turned upside down, trashed and destroyed what our Forefathers and so many men and woman past and present sacrificed and shed their blood to hand us. We took a nation that grew faster than any other on planet earth, created more wealth in 150 years from its inception than all other nations combined, and we successfully turned it into a debtor nation, unable to financially survive for much longer, and we did this in less than a century.

Democracy: Did you ever wonder why if democracy is so good, how come we don't run our businesses or indeed our very households under democratic rule? The answer is simple, it will not work! If we ran our businesses and our homes under a democratic philosophy, all of our businesses and our households (at least households with dependents) would all go broke. Imagine sitting down to the table each month with your kids and setting up your budget were everyone in the family gets a vote on how the monthly income will be utilized. Or, how long do you think your business (or any business for that matter) would last if all the employees got to vote on their own wage increases and how all the company profits should be spent. In either our homes or our businesses, our success would be held hostage to those who would make their decisions based on their own wants and needs, and not on that which would be beneficial to either our households or our companies. Democracy in the home or the work place would mean certain failure.

So why then do we think it would work for a government? The simple answer is that under our current rules that govern our form of democracy it won't. Just like the examples of our homes or our business, when you give people the right to vote that have no skin in the game (are not tax-paying or retired tax paying citizens) democracy will fail and fail miserably. It is human nature unfortunately. Most people when given the opportunity will simply ask for more if they can gain more personally with little or no thought to how it may impact the whole. Even if they know that the pot will run dry, until that time they will take as much as they can simply because they can. If given the choice to have whatever you want in life without having to work for it, what would you do? Unfortunately, we have a huge portion of our society in America that lives exactly that way. Their idea of what they want in life is to simply exist.

It is possible that a society could include in its democracy the right to vote for even those who are not taxpayers, if the portion of non-tax-paying voters was a relatively small percentage in comparison to tax-paying voters. However as you grow the pot of dependency so do you grow the base of non-tax-paying voters. Not only do you grow that particular base, but you accelerate the growth of this group over time. Our current economic philosophy guarantees this. In-fact every socialist economic philosophy guarantees this. The only way a democracy can work is if the economic philosophy in that society is one of *capitalism*.

There must be a philosophy of *free markets* coupled with strict limits on *government intervention*. This is the only philosophy that limits and reduces both poverty as well as the pool of non-tax-paying citizens to a minimum.

The Socialist States of America

The United States of America is a *socialist* nation. While the vast majority of Americans, from our common citizenry to our politicians, will argue that we are a *capitalist* society, the plain truth is that we are socialist. We have been socialist for a good while. While there are many people today that like to blame the State of our Union on capitalism, the fact of the matter is that socialism is to blame for the state we find ourselves in today. Historically, we can trace the beginnings of the decline of America to the infusion of socialism into our economy and as we increased the rate of socialism we equally increased the rate of decline.

Anti-capitalists like to point to both the economic and social decline in America to the evils of capitalism. They eagerly point fingers at big business accusing them of making to much profit, or they will blame capitalism for the disparity in incomes between the top earners and the low earners. They will hold this philosophy accountable for the increasing poverty levels in the nation and they will bash freedom and free markets as if these are the cause for a weak economy and lack of meaningful jobs. What they really don't understand is that it is a mathematical and historical fact that these are the effects of socialism. To understand this, one must first know something of the philosophies of socialism and capitalism, the latter commonly referred to as *Laissez Faire*, or "free from government intervention". Once you have some knowledge of the two different philosophies, you can then compare how our government has ruled over the past century and better understand which of the two philosophies they have been governing by.

The Basics of the Socialist Philosophy

Socialism is an economic philosophy that uses central planning to govern the economy. It is a philosophy or belief that a government, through careful central planning and manipulation, can control the nation's economic outcome. In a socialist nation, the government controls the financial strings of the economy and in doing so, it controls all aspects of the economy. In a socialist economy, economic growth is dependent on government spending. The government controls what parts of the economy to prop up with the anticipation of creating growth in the selected sectors in which they infuse money. This is called *stimulus*. The government controls the money supply for the nation. It creates the rules that businesses are allowed to operate under, dictates how money can be borrowed, and at what interest rate. It either regulates through central planning every aspect of the economy, or it takes direct ownership of the nations resources and businesses. Socialist advocates believe that by doing so, they can strike a balance averting huge swings in the economic boom bust cycles (the business cycle) while at the same time providing for a financial equal landscape for the common citizenry. On the outside, socialism touts the belief that through government intervention, it can more evenly divide the wealth of the nation. The theory is that their citizens will have a more equal take, reducing poverty by usurping from the productive sectors of the economy to donate to the nonproductive sectors. This, however, has never proved to be true and has only served to simply reduce the overall nations wealth and increase the poverty levels. Socialism skews the natural laws of economics and for all intents and purposes actually reverses or turns upside down those laws, in effect reversing the engine.

Some of the most noted economists that touted and implemented these economic philosophies were Vladimir Lenin (Russian economist who implemented his theories on the Russian economy in 1917), Karl Marx (German Economist/Philosopher whose socialist and or communist philosophies had a profound impact on both Russia in 1922 and Communist China in 1942). John Maynard Keynes (British economist whose socialist economic theories of *central economic planning* were implemented in Europe and the United States during the Franklin Delano Roosevelt administration and are followed by our government to this day).

The Basics of the Capitalist Philosophy

Capitalism (Laissez-faire) is an economic philosophy with principles that are exactly the opposite of socialism. Capitalism is a system in which the economy and all of its components are best left to the will or freedom of the citizens of a nation. This environment leaves the *natural* laws of economics to the tendencies of the overall population of the nation. In other words, the economy moves up and down based on the wants, needs, production and consumption habits of the people. Capitalism or the *Laissez-faire* economic approach fosters the idea that there should be minimal interference from the government and no *central* planning. A *free people* and their way of life should dictate the growth or retraction of the overall economy.

Capitalist believe that under this philosophy, the nation as a whole would become a wealthier nation by the natural results of freedom. Through capitalism its citizens would have less poverty and it would allow for an equal footing for every member of the nation through their dedication to creating wealth via their own labor. The consept of capitalism is that it would allow citizens the opportunity to continue to increase wealth for themselves and their future generations without limit. When left unhindered, the fulfillment of creating wealth at the individual level would create wealth for the entire nation.

Some of the most noted philosophers and economists that supported this philosophy was Thomas Jefferson, Adam Smith and Alexander Hamilton. They instituted these economic policies in America at our founding and by doing so laid the foundation for the United States of America to become an economic power house. Thus, creating more wealth and becoming the wealthiest nation on the planet in less than one hundred fifty years. Not only did the United States become the wealthiest nation on planet earth, but it surpassed the wealth and productive capacity of all other nations combined. Historically this tremendous trend of creating both personal and national wealth continued to accelerate up to, and for a short period beyond our fundamental change in economic philosophy from capitalism to socialism.

Once one has a basic understanding of the two philosophies, it becomes easier to see by simply researching history and having a basic understanding of math, when and how the United States of America converted from a free capitalist economy to a government controlled socialist economy. It becomes much easier to understand that all the many arguments that capitalism is the reason for all of our economic problems is every bit attributed to socialism and not capitalism. Under the socialist philosophy, the prevalence of increased poverty, increased welfare, increased government dependency, increased government debt, devalued currency, government deficits, fiscal cliffs, and increased cost of living all contribute to the moral decay of our nation.

All of these economic ills started within 30 years of the ground work being laid to implement socialism (during the Woodrow Wilson administration in the early 1900s) and the decline was accelerated once the United States of America changed its economic philosophy to total socialism in the 1930s during the Roosevelt administration.

Are We Really a Socialist Nation?

Without a doubt, for over one hundred years we have been a socialist nation. You don't need to take my word for it when the answer is right there in front of you. To simplify it however, let's just take a look at how our economy operated over the last century up to and including today.

Today, our economy is totally driven by government spending. You may not know this and if you don't, you are actually a part of the largest group of Americans today. If you have any doubt that the United States economy is one hundred percent dependent on government spending, all you need to do is walk over to your T.V. set and turn on a news channel. It doesn't matter what news channel, conservative, liberal, or main stream. Any news channel will do. Listen for these key words and phrases:

- **Fiscal Cliff:** this is term that describes when the Government is in constant contention between Democrat and Republican parties as to *if* or *how* the *debt ceiling* should be raised to avert economic disaster. If the economy wasn't dependent on government spending then there would be no fiscal cliff and therefore no pending disaster.
- **The Markets:** (stock markets) are responding to either a compromise or lack of one in Congress over the budget. In an economy not being controlled by the government the markets respond to...well, market forces, such as if a company is making a *profit* and paying a *dividend*. The stock market today primarily moves up and down based on what the government will or will

not do when it comes to spending or stimulating the economy. It will move based on what is happening in other countries as well, depending on what those governments can or cannot do to keep their economies propped up via government programmers' and spending. The stock market today is held hostage to the willingness or the ability of our governments to spend more and or keep their promise to pay their debts.

- **Inflation:** This is when the government decides to print money to cover for the shortfall in either tax receipts or the amount they borrow to pay for all of the programs or spending to keep the nation going. *This only takes place in socialist nations.* This does not always take place in all socialist nations, but it never takes place in nations that have adopted capitalism as the economic philosophy. However, introducing inflation into a capitalistic society always serves to accelerate the change in economic philosophy from capitalism to socialism.
- **Entitlements:** Entitlements are a result of socialism.
- **National Debt:** This is the amount of debt that the government owes to both *"we the people"* as well as some very unsavory countries like China. This is a debt that mathematically we can never pay. Once the government loses the ability to pay the debt, it will create both a national and worldwide depression on the scale that mankind has never ever seen. Absent of war, national debt is rarely experienced under a capitalist society. However, it is always found under a socialist society. In a capitalist society, the government is not normally allowed to accrue debt. It is limited to spending only what it receives. In a capitalist nation, the government's responsibility is limited by-and-large to the defense of the nation and ensuring that equality is guaranteed when it comes to economic and social freedoms.

This is historically paid for in the receipts from a small property tax paid into the government coffers by its citizenry.

- **Federal Reserve:** This is the privately owned banking system set up in 1913 and approved by Woodrow Wilson to centralize the nation's banks. This was one of the first steps needed to change the American economy from capitalist to socialist and is the birth-date for the socializing of America. Anytime you walk into your bank and see a sign that says "FDIC" insured, it should remind you that you are living in a socialist country. The **Federal Reserve**, or the **FED** as it is commonly called today, is at the forefront of centralized government planning. It dictates interest rates on money borrowed, controls the money supply, and mandates inflation, all the things that you will never find in a capitalist society and only in a socialist society.

"The Federal Reserve is a conglomerate of very wealthy private bankers that the United States Government by law turned over full control of both our money and banking systems. One of the most ungodly and fraudulent institutions ever perpetrated on the American people and the world, is the Federal Reserve System which through deceit became the central bank of the United States in 1913. The idea came about on a meeting in Jekyll Island off the coast of Georgia in 1910. The bankers in this country, especially J.P. Morgan, created a currency panic in 1907 in order to get the American people to accept the idea of a central bank."

- Dr. Ken Matto in his description of the Federal Reserve, in his writings titled: The Federal Reserve: History of Lies, Thievery, and Deceit

These are just a few key words and phrases that you can listen to for help in understanding what type of economic philosophy the United States of America is currently under.

Here is a litmus test you can use to determine if we are socialist or capitalist:

- Does our Government inflate the currency? Yes, Socialism
- Does the amount of money our Government spends dictate the health of the Nation's Economy? Yes, Socialism
- Does our Government regulate the economy? Yes, Socialism
- Does our Government regulate the Banks? Yes, Socialism
- Does our Government Centrally plan for Economic expansion? Yes, Socialism
- Does our Government redistribute wealth? Yes, Socialism
- Does our Government dictate interest rates? Yes, Socialism
- Does our Government regulate business? Yes, Socialism

So, let me reiterate we are not and have not been for one hundred years now, a nation with an economy that is capitalist. Capitalism is a system *free* from government intervention. Our current system is one hundred percent dependent on government intervention and spending. This doesn't mean that the government has to spend an equal amount annually compared to the GNP (Gross National Product). It simply means that the amount it spends is required to prevent either a recession or a depression. It means that if it stops spending or even cuts the amount it is spending, that the economy will start to decline, and without further spending (stimulus), the entire economy will fail. It means that if it continues to spend via inflation that it will continue to debauch the currency, reducing its value until it becomes worthless and a depression will occur. We became a socialist nation with the inception of the Federal Reserve during Wilson and we successfully converted our economic philosophy from capitalism (*free from government intervention*) which is the philosophy of our Founding Fathers, to that of socialism (*an economy driven by central planning*) touted by John Maynard Keynes and put into action by Franklin Delano Roosevelt in the 1930s.

Based on written history, the nationalizing of our banking system and the adoption of *Keynesian economics*, coupled with the documented philosophies that teach us the difference between capitalism and socialism, this is a point in my opinion that cannot even be argued. You can attempt to argue that socialism is better than capitalism, but I find it difficult to find a valid argument that for the last one hundred years that the United States of America has been anything other than a full blown socialist nation. She is a nation whose economy is centrally planned and controlled by her government. To blame anything that has occurred over the last one hundred years on the effects of capitalism to me is absolutely inaccurate and absurd.

Why is it important to understand this?

It is important to understand these things because in our country there is a great level of misunderstanding when it comes to the most important decisions that we have to make for the future of our nation. I have already expanded on my thoughts as to why there is this level of misunderstanding in this writing, and you too should be able at this point to either see this to be true, or at least have a need to investigate this further.

We see today many of our fellow Americans bashing capitalism, yet they have no idea that this philosophy is not at all responsible for the things they hold it accountable for. They do not realize that the contempt they have for our current economic philosophy is rooted in socialism and not capitalism. They simply do not understand that the philosophy that they currently call for (socialism) is the exact same philosophy responsible for the problems that not only our nation, but the very problems that many others nations find themselves facing today. We hear the term *Crony Capitalism* thrown around to describe a tainted form of capitalism responsible for the ills of our nation, when in fact *capitalism* in this nation ceased to exist in any form eighty years ago. Socialism and socialism alone is one hundred percent responsible for the economic problems we face today as a nation. We need an army of people to believe, to understand, and to shout loudly:

WE HAVE BEEN A ***SOCIALIST*** NATION FOR ONE HUNDRED YEARS! ***SOCIALISM*** IS THE REASON WE ARE IN DEBT AS A NATION AND ***SOCIALISM*** IS THE VERY REASON WE HAVE BECOME A SOCIETY IN WHICH POVERTY IS INCREASING AT AN UNSUSTAINABLE LEVEL! **NOT** *CAPITALISM*!

It was the very fact that for one hundred fifty years under a capitalist philosophy, that we were able to build a nation wealthy and strong enough, to absorb the evils of socialism up until now. If we hadn't become such a wealthy nation during those years we would have never been able to survive the effects of socialism for as long as we have without becoming a full on communist nation. Much of the world has been surviving on what we, the American people initially created in terms of wealth under a capitalist society well over one hundred years ago.

You cannot fix what you don't know to be broken. Equally, you cannot correct what you do not know to be wrong. The battle for America is not Democrat or Republican. In my opinion, neither party is really doing what is necessary to save our nation today.

While I am a financial conservative, to me the current Republican Party lacks the backbone to accomplish what needs to take place to save our nation from the throws of socialism and the eventual collapse into communism. The Democratic Party on the other hand, has been the primary catalyst that has changed our nation's economic philosophies and policies to that of socialism and has been the primary driver for escalating our path as a socialist nation. The bottom line is that we have to stop thinking along party lines. Neither of the two parties currently, have the will or character to do anything for "We the people." Our only hope is to become aware ourselves and then to educate and to assist our fellow Americans to remove their government imposed blinders.

There are few Americans alive today that have experienced a country whose economic philosophy is capitalism. Those that have seen this are over one hundred years old and would have been way too young to even remember it. Today, we are faced with virtually an entire citizenry that has grown up in this socialist culture. They are absolutely unaware of the difference between nations built on the philosophy of capitalism vs. the socialist society that they have been born into. If you don't think I am right, then I beg you to prove me wrong. While I have written about the basic philosophies here, I urge you to take the time to look up *capitalism* and just spend a few hours reading about this philosophy, then spend a couple hours reading about the philosophy *socialism*. I promise, this doesn't take years of study and the knowledge is not limited to historians or economists. Bump what you discover against the current practices that you see taking place every single day in America perpetuated by her government.

Banking Conceived in Iniquity

"Banking was conceived in iniquity and was born in sin. The bankers own the earth. Take it away from them, but leave them the power to create money, and with the flick of the pen they will create enough deposits to buy it back again. However, take it away from them, and all the great fortunes like mine will disappear and they ought to disappear, for this would be a happier and better world to live in. But, if you wish to remain the slaves of bankers and pay the cost of your own slavery, let them continue to create money."

Sir Josiah Stamp, Director of the Bank of England (appointed 1928). Reputed to be the 2nd wealthiest man in England at that time

The bankers will own everything and the government will be their subordinate to enforce the forfeiture of personal property, whether it is our guns, homes, business or real money such as gold and silver. People don't think that this can happen here, but let's remember that just eighty years ago during the last Great Depression, our government confiscated all the real money (**gold**) from the population making it illegal for citizens to own. The government told the people that by having a gold-backed currency that it was hindering the growth of the nation. People discounted the historical fact that while the nation had been on the gold standard for the previous one hundred years, that America became the most prosperous nation on the planet. People back then thought that this request to take their gold and turn it in for the Federal Reserve's paper money was for the good of their country. They believed that our government needed the gold. What they never asked though was why did the government need their wealth that they saved in the form of gold, when they took the dollars they were giving in exchange for their gold off the gold standard at the same time? It was one of the greatest heists of all time. It almost makes me laugh whenever I think of how the Federal Reserve pulled that off. Of course you can own gold now, at least for the meantime, but I will tell you this: all the people who were forced by law to turn in their gold for the currency of the FED, never had the opportunity to buy their gold back using the same number of dollars that the FED gave them when they took their gold. It was and remains to this day, the greatest gold robbery in history. You only see Wild West movies depicting men riding into towns and stealing the gold from the banks. We missed the movie that showed the banks riding into town to steal the gold from an entire nation.

We've all heard the term leveraging other people's money to make money. This is exactly what the FED did. These wealthy bankers without using a dime of their own money bought the United States of America, her government and all of her inhabitants. They did this with a printing press and a concept and without a nickel of their own wealth. They stole the gold from all the citizens in the 1930s and replaced real money with nothing more than paper. It was the most brilliant gold robbery in human history and one in which the victims handed over their wealth willingly without the threat from a knife or a gun to the thieves. Could they or would they do this again during the next Great Depression? I will leave that to your own imagination.

What few Americans realize today, is that in a truly free economy, one free from government intervention, one that uses *real* money vs. *fake fiat* money, prices rarely if ever go up and the value of the money rarely if ever goes down. Just the opposite is true. The value of your money goes up against all other goods and services. In a *free* or *capitalistic* economy, people produce (create wealth) at a significantly higher rate as they vie for the available *limited real money*. Remember money, real money, is the measurement of wealth but not wealth in and of itself. There is no limit to wealth while there is a limit to real money. Wealth is what we produce in terms of goods; money is the measure by which we can trade for those goods.

In a *free* economy the fact that real money i.e. *gold* or *silver* is limited, is what actually stimulates the economy. People work harder, produce more, invent more and create more. They use their minds more to come up with ingenious ways to compete for the available money supply. Just like *socialism* reverses the engine of economics, fake fiat inflated money, reverses the relationship of money to goods and services.

I have listened to countless opinions from *Keynesian* trained economists who consistently present arguments that the dollar really hasn't devalued and that incomes have increased comparably to the rate of inflation. They work up their math and present their charts with *inflation adjusted* numbers and spend countless hours trying to convince themselves and others that *inflation* hasn't hindered but helped the economy. It's rather amusing really as they present their case which is nothing short of arguing that *"you can have your cake and eat it too"*. Their thought process is no different than that if you eat the cake, once it passes through your system the chemical makeup of the cake is still there. Ask them to eat the cake in its new state and none will reach for a fork. Facts are facts, and you can play with the math and make pretty charts all day long, but the fact remains that over the last several decades, we are a nation in constant financial crisis. The middle class is being methodically squeezed out, the welfare rolls continue to increase, our purchasing power continues to diminish, our national, corporate and consumer debt is mathematically beyond the measure of recovery and NONE of this is due to the lack of *inflating* the currency. As I listen too many of these *educated* people defend the current system, I find myself wanting to reach out and gently tap on their foreheads with a hammer, to get them to just for a moment stop their madness and simply look at the current state of the union. It's as if they have entered a maze and since they couldn't find their way out they have learned to love the maze, succumb to it and defend it.

8

BY ACCIDENT OR DESIGN THE END KNOWS NO DIFFERENCE

"I am a most unhappy man. I have unwittingly ruined my country. A great industrial nation is controlled by its system of credit. Our system of credit is concentrated. The growth of the nation, therefore, and all our activities are in the hands of a few men. We have come to be one of the worst ruled, one of the most completely controlled and dominated governments in the civilized world. No longer a government by free opinion, no longer a government by conviction and the vote of the majority, but a government by the opinion and duress of a small group of dominant men". - Woodrow Wilson

Even the President of the United States in 1913, the man responsible for signing into law the Federal Reserve Act that placed our nations financial future in the hands of a few private bankers, knew that in the end he set the foundation for

destroying our nation. Not only Wilson, but many congressmen, senators and all the bankers involved knew that they were sealing the fate of the American people. Equally, the men that have manipulated, pilfered, and robbed the wealth of this nation have known exactly what they have been doing from that time forward.

Over the last one hundred years, a handful of men have dictated and controlled through the manipulation of a private banking system both the United States government and the American people. Through finance, they have infiltrated our economy and the American way of life. **This is Treason!** I would welcome the opportunity to stand in front of any court in this land and plead this case.

"Because the privately owned Federal Reserve Bank of New York sets interest rates and controls the daily supply of price of currency throughout America, the owners of that bank are the real directors of that whole system. These shareholders have controlled our political and economic destinies since 1913."
— Eustace Mullins, Secrets of the Privately Owned Federal Reserve

"The money trust deliberately caused the 1907 money panic and thereby forced Congress to create a National Monetary Commission which led to the ultimate creation of the privately owned FederalReserve Bank. The Federal Reserve Act establishes the most gigantic monetary trust on earth. When the President signs the bill, the invisible government of the Monetary Powers will be legalized. The people must make a declaration of independence to relieve

themselves from the Monetary Powers, by taking control of Congress!... The worst legislative crime of the ages is perpetrated by this banking bill. The caucus and the party bosses have again operated and prevented the people from getting the benefit of their own government!"

—Congressman Charles Lindbergh Sr. (stated the day before the Federal Reserve Act was passed)

"If this mischievous financial policy (of creating a debt-free currency), which has its origin in the American Republic, shall become permanent, then that government will furnish its own money without cost! It will pay off its debts and be without debt. It will have all the money to carry on its commerce. It will become prosperous without precedent in the history of the world. The brains and the wealth of all countries will go to America. That government must be destroyed or it will destroy every monarchy on the globe!"

—(An editorial that appeared in the London times owned by the Rothschild Banking Dynasty during the time that President Lincoln was taking action to create the United States own currency).

I find it impossible to believe that the bankers and many politicians in 1913, did not know exactly what they were doing. Those men then, no different then the bankers along with many of our current politicians today are highly educated, and pleading ignorance is absolutely absurd. The fact that they knew then and continue to know now how to do this is a testament to their knowledge of both history and math. History, because it had been done before, and not just that others had done it before them, but the family-tree of some of the bankers that own the Federal Reserve had done this to nations before ours. Then, math because if you can simply add, subtract, divide and you are a banker, than you know exactly what the results will be from using this recipe. There is no doubt, that these few men and their families unleashed a philosophy and inserted the tools necessary to steal the wealth of the greatest nation on the planet earth. Math is math and I just cannot fathom that bankers and politicians at the turn of the twentieth century did not know exactly what nationalizing the banks, inflating the currency and instituting the overarching social programs would do to the nation over time. In my opinion this was done with full intent and with malice. In so doing they intentionally created an atmosphere in which the only government that was truly designed to be *"by and for the people,"* would fill itself to the brim with like-minded-evil-men, intent on stealing what they considered their share of the peoples wealth as the bankers increased their personal fortunes and power on the backs of the American people.

Hiding the True Tax Rate

Inflation and government borrowing hides the level of a citizen's true tax rate

Ending inflation would instantly change the minds of both Republican and Democrat tax paying citizens, creating a power house for change. If it wasn't for inflation and if all things in our economy remained exactly like they are today, the taxpaying portion of our citizens would have to be taxed at an **eighty percent tax rate** just to sustain our current level of government spending. It's simple math. If you take a look at the governments current annual spending, and then you look at the total income of our population and consider the percent of people that actually pay taxes in our nation, you can easily figure out how much of our income we would have to give our Federal government so that they can continue to spend at their current rate.

Governments use inflation to hide the level of taxation that they are placing on their citizens. Oddly enough, this form of taxation knows no class. Americans believe that we live in a country that if you make a low level of income (that level set by the government) that you do not pay Federal income tax. That however is one of the biggest deceptions by our government on the American people. Rich or poor, inflation robs you of your purchasing power. The only ones that benefit from this is the government. It's a trick in accounting if you will. The only purpose being to conceal from the public the amount of taxes that they are truly paying to keep the government afloat.

Therefore, if we stopped both inflation and government borrowing, how long do you think it would take the taxpaying citizenry to wake up and change both who they allow to govern them and the economic philosophy that has created this mess? When you think about it, that is really what all of our nations problems boil down to. We are plagued with an uninformed citizenry, dumbed down by government intervention that over the years has hid with great success, what it has been doing to its people in the interest of self-preservation. Do you think it would take one year, five years, or a decade at an eighty percent tax rate? Or, do you think it would take one or two paychecks? Ending inflation alone would be the single thing that would wake up our nation so very quickly so that change could be forced virtually overnight.

Another question should be, if we can successfully end inflation and we refused to pay taxes at the rate needed to cover the current government spending, what would that do to the economy? The answer: It would cause a deflationary depression necessary to correct one hundred years of deceit, deception, and the conversion to socialism. There is going to be a depression without a doubt, and once again, one type is better than the other. One could lead us back to freedom, while the other will lead us to slavery.

The next question, what if we end inflation and we decide to go ahead and pay the exorbitant tax necessary to keep the country going while we reduced the governments spending? The answer: We would still suffer a *deflationary* depression. You can't take eighty percent of spendable income out of the private sector without causing a depression.

And the final question should be, What if we do nothing at all and just continue the way we are going? The answer: hyperinflation, the worst depression of the two will occur. It's just simply a matter of time. This has been documented time and time again throughout the history of banks and governments attempting to control a nations economy. Our nation is not the first to have its currency inflated. What you need to know and understand is the end result will be the same, with the exception that our hyper-inflationary depression will be many times worse than any in previous history. This is simply because we have incorporated or exported our inflation to many of the other nations in our world. We have made most other countries dependent on our spending and when the *devil comes to roost*, and he will, this hyper-inflationary depression will be on a scale never before seen in history. To me, this is not an option. However, it appears that the odds of this type of depression occurring are much higher than having a deflationary depression. A deflationary depression would allow us to recover relatively quickly, restore our foundation and begin to grow on sound footing, leaving a better nation for our future generations. The chances however, that the American people will stand up and force our government into doing what is best for the nation is an amazing stretch.

Inflation; Creating Chaos Abroad

The use of inflation in the United States hasn't just impacted our nation. As a matter of fact, the United States exported our inflation to many nations without warning or forethought. The fact is that the inflation perpetuated by the United States via the World bankers that own the Federal Reserve has had an adverse impact not just on our own citizens, but on the citizens of many other nations as well.

If we take just one subject, foreign policy, and we ask ourselves without political eyes how things became so convoluted in these foreign countries? Why is it that we are dependent on foreign oil when it is apparently so abundant beneath our own feet? Why is it that there is so much hatred, animosity and ill will towards us the American people, who for argument sake give so much to these nations that hate us? While both the Democrats and the Republicans equally spend untold resources and energy spinning their views in the foreign political arena, neither party will tell the truth nor do what is necessary to take the appropriate measures to correct what historically is our government's own doing. This is not to insinuate that it is the American people's fault for the ill will in many other nations towards us. To me, over the years the American people and the American government have become two very different parts of our society. That said, since it is the American people that cast the votes for those that represent us, many foreigner's will hold the American people responsible for the actions of our government regardless of the deception that has been perpetuated on the American voter.

I will concede that there is a religious factor that obviously has spawned a deadly foe as well. But, let's not forget that Christianity at one time in our history was just as deadly to those that opposed its beliefs. The difference here is that today, the technology to decimate entire populations is available making the fanatics of the present-day a thousand fold more deadly than the fanatics of the past. This is equally an effect of inflation. The one single issue that neither major political party will address in a manner in which to resolve. Stick with me and I will make my case for this and you can decide for yourself. In fact you may find that it is the first time you can actually decide for yourself given the untold fog that exists today.

A bit of history: Inflating the currency in foreign lands.

In order to understand how inflation could possibly be responsible for these claims, you have to understand how we transported our decision to inflate our currency, to inflating the currency of many other nations. What the American socialist did occurred without warning or forethought to what it would do to other nations economies. This is the root cause, or effect, of almost all the issues we currently face as it pertains to foreign policy and foreign issues.

In the 1930s, Roosevelt took Americans off the Gold standard internally, but left the dollar pegged to gold for foreigners. Prior to Roosevelt making this historical change to our currency, the dollar was backed by a fixed amount of gold. Once Roosevelt took us off the gold standard internally, the government tried to maintain that a dollars value was equal to 1/35th of an ounce of gold. Theoretically, foreign nations could still turn in the US dollars they held for that fixed amount. Many foreign nations actually held the US dollar in their own treasuries and then printed their nations currencies with the US dollar to back them. It was easier and more convenient to hold the paper dollar redeemable by gold then to hold physical gold in their own vaults. This trust in America would prove to be a decision that would be detrimental to their economic health as seen during the Nixon administration.

So, along comes the Nixon administration, were the decision (no doubt at the behest of the bankers) was made to remove the dollar from the gold standard even to foreign nations. This act transported our inflation to any nation that was holding US dollars to back their own currency, as well as any foreign trader holding US dollars literally overnight. In one fell swoop, these nations who used the US dollar to back their own currency (*because theoretically they could exchange those dollars for a fixed amount of gold from the Federal Reserve*), suddenly woke up one morning to find their currency worth-less than what it was just the night before. Even foreign nations that traded in US dollars (since it was then and still is the *world reserve* currency), suddenly found that the dollars they held to effect trade with other nations, had less value than the day before. Everyone suddenly had to ask for more dollars for their products because the dollars they traded with devalued overnight.

Hm-mm, I often wonder if the shoe was on the other foot, if we would have been a little irritated by that decision. Imagine waking up one day and all the prices of food and goods in our country doubled because of what another nation did. Nonetheless, there was as one can imagine many effects from this inflationary decision. This move corresponded with several major trade issues that cropped up as a result from exporting our inflation. Prices spiked due to the realization of the sudden inflation, causing a vast number of effects that are to this day very relevant both domestically and within our never ending *trade balance* issues. So the race was on in the 1970s to shore up all the ill effects of the inflation we exported. One of the many decisions made, was to reduce the tax required on some foreign goods entering our country to try and make up, or for a better word, appease our foreign friends for inflating the currency they used to trade. Those tax-breaks were the direct *cause* from that inflationary effect that led to us becoming dependent on foreign oil.

It became more profitable due to our own governments meddling with inflating our currency and the decisions they made to hide the *effects* of these terrible monetary decisions (reduce the tax on foreign oil making domestic oil more costly)for our own oil corporations to go foreign and import oil, than to continue to produce domestically. So, what are some of the *effects* of this bit of *inflationary* history?

The influx of American oil investment into the Middle East was unprecedented. Suddenly, nations whose populations primarily lived in tents or mud huts, with horse and camel as their means of transportation, and swords and pistol as their means of defense, were being modernized at a rate never before seen in history by American oil corporations. Instead of a culture left alone to continue to developing over time, entire nations were thrown into the modern world virtually overnight. Nations that by any modern thinking man would agree, less sophisticated when it came to religion and culture found themselves in a world that they were ill prepared for. Imagine handing the war mongering Christians of old the technology we possess today. Does any thinking person believe that there would be anyone left on the planet but Christians? We created much of the chaos that is coming home to roost in America today and if one were to really take an interest and look, the majority of our issues stem from, or are a direct *cause and effect* of our own *inflation*.

History teaches us that we will not survive as a free nation if we continue to inflate our currency. Both Republicans and Democrats know this, yet neither party has the will to resolve this all important issue. I can easily tie the majority of the real issues this nation faces back to the inflation or debasement of our currency. And don't be fooled, so can many of our political leaders. Welfare, social security solvency, unemployment, the never ending cycle of prices and the cost of living going up, the national debt, the deficit, health-care expenses, lack of jobs and the list goes on and on, all of these issues have one common underlying cause and that is inflation.

As a nation, by-and-large, we would rather focus on the effects of the cancer eroding our lives than to focus on the cause of the cancer itself. This, friends, is yet another effect of inflation. Both of our major political parties would rather us focus on being against one another over the issues of fog. They would rather us focus on issues such as marriage equality, or if a woman has the right to do what she wants with her own body, or if one party has more of an affinity to helping the downtrodden, or if one party philosophy is more able to strengthen the ever declining economy thereby increasing our standard of living. Both parties are equally responsible for where the U.S. and frankly much of the world finds itself today.

From the progressive liberal Woodrow Wilson and the democratically elected Franklin D Roosevelt who set the foundation for our downfall, to the Republican Richard Nixon and on up through to our current President, every administration and every congress is responsible for perpetuating the inflation that erodes the fiber of this nation. None are willing to tell the truth, because frankly, the truth would set us free (of them anyway). Today's leaders will mention inflation from time to time, but none of them are willing to truly educate the population and prepare us for what measures need to be taken to overcome it. None of them will talk to us about what will ultimately be the end result if we do not.

So, in the end, who is really responsible? We are. The American people who will vote without education. We who know but yet refuse to educate, participate, or speak out, to ensure that more can understand. Staunch believers of both parties spend more time and energy today, accusing those that oppose them of drinking the proverbial kool-aid. Spitting words of hatred at one another falling prey to the disgusting political perpetrators of both parties, while all the while marching in step to the madness, entering the ever thickening fog spewed from the majority of our leaders entrusted with our well-being.

Economics

Economics is not a hard subject to understand, unless you make the mistake and study it.

"*An invisible hand guides the economy to reach its most efficient method of meeting and creating supply and demand of goods and services.*"
-Adam Smith, *Wealth of Nations*

What Adam Smith was saying, is that there is nothing required, no outside force, no amount of manipulation or intervention to ensure a healthy robust economy. The rules of economics are so very simple and when left alone (*Capitalism*), the natural laws of economics fair very well. In a capitalistic, *Laissez Faire*, environment, the engine of economics is fueled by the way we live. Our consumption creates demand, our demand creates production and our production creates wealth. It is truly that simple and to study it further will not change the *natural laws* of economics. However, when you interfere with the natural laws of economics by introducing socialism, you actually reverse those very laws. Socialism, through central government planning, takes our wealth and spends it to create production, in attempts to create demand, in an attempt to create our wants and needs or consumption. It turns the natural laws of economics upside down reversing the engine, just as if you reversed the polarity on an electric motor (causing it to run in reverse). In doing so it has destroyed our wealth and increased our debt. Sound familiar?

The study of economics today is easily convoluted by the vast amount of literature out there that seeks to understand how to control inflation. Over the years, many economist, politicians, philosophers and political science majors find themselves lost as they continue to delve into the study of economics. They get caught up in the *Keynesian web*, and mentally get entangled in all of the many remedies and writings designed to either attempt to understand or control a system burdened by inflation. Unfortunately, some either never understand or they lose sight of the big picture getting caught up in the man-made-maze that our current economic system has created. Then there are others who fully understand and they either find themselves fighting for truth and freedom, or lining up with those who would benefit themselves at the cost of freedom.

Economic Philosophies

By its nature, capitalism is the only philosophy that requires no government to enforce it. When studying different economic philosophies, it is difficult sometimes to weed through the muddle in order to determine which one might be more beneficial to a nation, or for that matter all of mankind. What I find most interesting is that all of the economic philosophers, no matter who they are or what philosophy they believe in, contemplate that theirs will deliver equality for the masses. They all believe that the nations that impose these philosophies will deliver to their citizen's utopian benefits. From Karl Marx, Vladimir Lenin, Adam Smith, Thomas Jefferson, Edmund Burke, Alexander Hamilton and John Maynard Keynes, they all believed that their philosophy would deliver equality and benefit nations.

If you take a look at both communism and socialism without the stigma that we like to attach to them, they have some very good concepts if a nation *freely* embraced and agreed to follow those practices. If for example; every person in China agreed to get up every morning and freely dedicate their day to producing for the benefit of their neighbor and nation, sharing equally in all that was produced distributed by their government, well... communism might just be a wonderful utopian state to be had. The exact same thing might hold true for socialism. The problem with both philosophies is that if every single person in the nation doesn't feel that they should produce for the benefit of their neighbor and that of the nation, then to attempt the philosophy it must be imposed by a government. There has never been a nation throughout history in which every member of a nation has *freely* accepted either of these philosophies. Throughout history, communism and socialism need governments to impose their philosophy on the people of their nations, and in every instance in which it has been imposed it has disincentivized the people of those nations and diminished the ability for that nation to produce enough wealth to advance their nations.

Out of the three most widely studied philosophies, capitalism is the only one that by its very nature **needs no enforcement** by a government. The only thing capitalism needs government for, is to ensure freedom and liberty and to protect the people *from* a government. If you believe in *freedom*, then to embrace either socialism or communism imposed by a government would be by its nature contrary to your beliefs. Both, by doctrine, use a government to enforce the philosophy on the nations that embrace them. Think about it for a moment, a nation of *free people* simply do not need a *government* to force them to be *free*.

The Founding Fathers of our nation were men wise beyond their times. By any measure, they were much smarter than those who consider themselves statesmen today. They understood that a people left to their freedom without government intervention would prosper, and they were absolutely right. They left us a nation and a constitution that prior to us altering and skirting around it, allowed our nation to create more wealth at a rate never before recorded in human history. If left unabated, the United States of America and all of its inhabitants would be light years ahead of where we are today.

Most people when thinking of socialism or communism conjure up images in their minds of governments dictating how their people live by military rule. There have been a number of nations that impose their philosophies just that way. We see through history governments that not only impose these economic philosophies, but at the same time take measures that prevent their citizens from opposing them. This is often done by a combination of military force and civil penalties imposed on their citizens to keep them in line with their philosophy. Many of these governments, Communist China, Russia, and North Korea to name a few, use government measures to censure and restrict what the people of their nations can read, write or even see or hear in their nationally controlled medias. What makes American socialism different today from those forms of socialism is our original constitution, which as of yet, hasn't been totally circumvented. Because of our constitution, America has in place socialism with freedom of speech as well as the right to bear arms. The question today is, will our democracy use these freedoms to save our nation from the philosophy of socialism, or will we use our democracy to allow the philosophy of socialism to take even these freedoms?

By the Sword or by Deceit Socialism is Socialism

Whether your freedom, liberties and wealth are taken by force or taken by deceit the end result knows no difference. There are only two forms of socialism that exist in our world today and neither type were *freely* embraced. We have nations in which socialism is forced like the former Union of Soviet Socialists Republics, known today as Russia and several of the satellite nations that surround it and then we have nations that have implemented socialism by means of deceit. The deceit to impose socialism for example on the people of the United States of America, has been so thorough and run so deep that by and large its inhabits don't even know that they are socialist.

One only has to understand the philosophies themselves without prejudice and bump those up against the economic practices that their government both embrace and impose. Whether socialism is imposed on the people of a nation or its government puts into practice methods that inflict its philosophy through deception, the end result knows no difference. Socialism does not produce! Socialism, in either form, destroys the wealth of its people and in doing so destroys the wealth of its nation. Socialism by its very nature creates poverty and in-debts a people to its government. There is not one single example throughout the written history of mankind that has proved otherwise. Yet every example in history supports the truth of this statement, every single one!

The United States will not be the first nation in history to overcome that fact, for to do so the laws of math would have to fall apart and be rendered useless. For the United States of America, and all socialist nations today, the debt of these nations alone are a testament to this fact. Math is the only true science known to man, and by any mathematical measure of any monetary system, *debt* is the exact opposite of both *savings* and *wealth*. It cannot be contested, that a nation that carries a public debt of near 17 *Trillion* dollars and as of 2012, 11.31 *Trillion* dollars in consumer debt along with 122 *Trillion* dollars in unfunded liabilities, is a nation light years removed from prosperity and wealth.

The Road to Hell is Paved with Good Intentions

Over the years I have had nearly an equal number of friends and acquaintances that consider themselves either *conservative* or *liberal* minded people. While they believe that their chosen political persuasion sets them apart from each other, I have come to the conclusion that by-and-large those outside of the political arena are of the same heart.

While great debate takes place between them on what is best for the nation and how to achieve it, the depth of deceit extolled by our government has equally taken a toll on *all*, no matter which philosophy is touted. Just like socialism and communism are concepts that if *freely* embraced by all could deliver the utopia they promise, liberals and conservatives are faced with a very similar scenario.

The divide, as I see it, is that liberals believe that it is a people's moral responsibility, to take care of those that cannot take care of themselves. They believe that there are a number of social programs that the people should support for the betterment of the nation as a whole. They believe that those who make more should pay more as a portion of the social programs they endorse, and if need be, should be forced to do so by law simply for the privilege of making their money in America.

Once again, most liberals that I know that are *not* politicians, simply want everyone to have a fair share and believe it is the taxpayers responsibility to give it to them. In summary, they do not like to see poor or underprivileged people and they truly want to do something about it.

Outside of economics, liberals have a belief of equality in social issues. For example; they believe that woman should have a right to an abortion and that gay people should have an equal right to marry who they want and be entitled to the same benefits of heterosexual marriages. When it comes to social issues, they want the government out of everyone's lives (*individual freedom*), but when it comes to economic issues they want the government involved in everyone's lives (*socialism*).

From an economic standpoint, it is not the final goal of the liberals that is a problem. It is the method to achieve it that is destructive and counterproductive to their own goals.

Conservatives like to think of themselves as the group of people that if the government would just follow their philosophies the nation would end up in a better place. They call for the government to balance the budget and they believe that the government is out of control when it comes to spending. They are not proponents of the welfare system and believe that it perpetuates poverty, but at the same time, they do not want to hear about the possible end to Social Security. They have an idea of what the government should cut in order to bring about some fiscal sanity, but they won't take all the measures necessary to make the corrections to save our nation.

Just like the liberals, conservative politicians will preach about their method to create jobs (an absolute socialist philosophy) while talking about getting the burden of government out of the way of the private sector. Conservatives say they believe in limited government when it comes to economic issues. But when it comes to social issues they want the government to rule over the morality of the nation. Yet, most conservatives that I know outside of the political arena are good hearted people who do not want to see people in poverty just like the liberal minded people. Their theory of achieving it is just different. They believe rightfully so that the welfare system keeps people poor and to continue to throw money at it will just grow the number of people in poverty and expand the welfare rolls. At the same time however, they will call for more government spending in areas like expanding the military, and will advocate for the government funding of infrastructure programs in the name of job creation.

One thing is for certain, whether it is Republican or Democrat, Liberal or Conservative, taxing, borrowing and inflating are used equally despite who is in control of the federal government. The national debt continues to rise, our purchasing power continues to diminish, the welfare rolls continue to increase and the standard of living continues to decline. Liberal or Conservative, they all have good intentions but believe me, "The road to hell is paved with good intentions," and we are well on our way to economic hell.

Effecting change can only be gotten by the willingness of individuals to take action. The way I see it, is that once you understand what has taken place and what needs to be done to correct it, you really only have two choices. You can become part of the solution and take action, or you can take no action and remain part of the problem.

9

What to Do

What to do, what to do, what to do....

Most Americans believe that the problems America faces are so insurmountable that there is nothing that one person can do to effect the kind of change necessary to stop the evil-take-over of our nation. However, the fact is everyone, no matter who, can do something. Knowledge is power and just one person can multiply that power by simply helping other Americans to understand what has taken place in our once great nation.

What has occurred in our nation is absolutely without a doubt intentional. Our wealth has been robbed, our access to knowledge has been robbed and our children's futures have not only been robbed but we have committed them to slavery. All of this made possible simply because we have been unaware of who the American socialist depression creators are and what they have been up to.

There is no question in my mind as to why they have done this, to me that is obvious. Each person involved, man or woman, be it the bankers that own the Federal Reserve, or the members of government that they control, possess the personality traits required that I mentioned at the beginning of this book.

It is easy to see who the politicians are both current and from the past, but the bankers have kept themselves well hidden, so let me tell you who they are and you can do some of your own research if you like. Here is a list of the Member Banks that control our lives both here in the United States and abroad:

Rothschild Bank of London, Warburg Bank of Hamburg, Rothschild Bank of Berlin, Lehman Brothers of New York, Lazard Brothers of Paris, Kuhn Loeb Bank of New York, Israel Moses Seif Banks of Italy, Goldman, Sachs of New York, Warburg Bank of Amsterdam, Chase Manhattan Bank of New York.

Originally, there was approximately 203,053 shares of privately owned Federal Reserve stocks at the FED's inception. Approximately 65% of those shares were owned by foreign banks while 35% were owned by the largest bankers here in the United States. While the Federal Reserve Act in 1913, includes as part of the act keeping these stock holders names a secret, there have been works by others that have overtime successfully revealed who they are. One of the best works was from R.E. McMaster, publisher of the newsletter "The Reaper" who discovered through Swiss banking connections, the banks that have controlling interest in the privately owned Federal Reserve.

Out of the 72,000 shares of the Federal Reserve owned by American banking investors, the best known breakdown was as follows.

* Rockefeller National City Bank = 30,000 shares
* Chase National = 6,000 shares (currently Chase Manhattan)
* The National Bank of Commerce = 21,000 shares (now known as Morgan Guaranty Trust)
* Morgan's First national Bank = 15,000 shares

So according to McMasters, the Morgans and the Rockefeller's are the American bankers that own thirty five percent of the Federal Reserve while foreigner's like the Rothschild's own the remainder. The point here is, the Federal Reserve IS NOT either owned by the American people or by the United States Government. It is owned by powerful bankers, yet we are forced by law to use it's currency, and are subject to it terms of lending and interest rates.

There are many people outside of the bankers themselves that seem to have a very keen interest in how not only our nation but how the entire world operates today. 1913, and the entire Wilson era was a historical pivotal point in time for the United States and the American citizen. Not only did the wealthiest bankers successfully take over the financial life blood of our nation, but Wilson in his infinite wisdom came up with and promoted an organization called the League of Nations. Created under the guise that this would be a platform designed to encourage cooperation and prevent aggression amongst nations. The Senate refused to grant Wilson's wish to become a member of this organization. Be that as it may, the League of Nations is an organization that Americans know today as the United Nations of which the United States is not only a member, but uses American soil to host this organization. Another organization that sprung up in our nation in 1973 was the Trilateral Commission. Oddly enough, The Rockefeller family (primary stock holder of the largest banks in our nation), had their hands in both these organizations. John D Rockefeller jr. financially supported the League of Nations and David Rockefeller was the actual founder of the Trilateral Commission. For better or worse, these organizations both past and present have been filled to the brim with actors that find the need to both control governments and the people of nations. Today, one such group that likes to get together and plot next steps for the world is the members of the highly secretive Bilderberg organization.

This is a partial list of some past and present American members who for some reason think it important that they get involved in an organization whose intent is one world government: hell-bent on creating a governing class, eliminating the middle class for that of a working class.

❊ Thomas E. Donilon (2012), Executive Vice President for Law and Policy at Fannie Mae (1999–2005), Current National Security Advisor for The White House.

- Roger Altman (2008, 2009), Deputy Treasury Secretary from 1993–1994, Founder and Chairman of Evercore Partners
- George W. Ball (1954, 1993), Under Secretary of State 1961–1968, Ambassador to U.N. 1968
- Sandy Berger (1999), National Security Advisor, 1997–2001
- Timothy Geithner (2008, 2009), Treasury Secretary
- Dick Gephardt (2012), former Congressman and House Majority Leader
- Lee H. Hamilton (1997), former Congressman
- Christian Herter, (1961, 1963, 1964, 1966), 53rd United States Secretary of State
- Charles Douglas Jackson (1957, 1958, 1960), Special Assistant to the President
- Joseph E. Johnson (1954), President Carnegie Endowment for International Peace
- Henry Kissinger (1957, 1964, 1966, 1971, 1973, 1974, 1977, 2008, 2009, 2010, 2011, 2012) 56th United States Secretary of State
- Mark G. Mazzie (1986, 1987), Chief of Staff, The Honorable George C. Wortley, U.S. House of Representatives.
- Richard Perle (2011), Chairman of the Defense Policy Board Advisory Committee 2001–2003, United States Assistant Secretary of Defense 1981–1987
- Colin Powell (1997), 65th United States Secretary of State

- Condoleezza Rice (2008), 66th United States Secretary of State
- George P. Shultz (2008), 60th United States Secretary of State
- Lawrence Summers, Director of the National Economic Council
- Paul Volcker[Chair of the President's Economic Recovery Advisory Board and Chairman of the Federal Reserve from 1979–1987
- Bing West (2010), author and former Assistant Secretary of Defense for International Security Affairs
- Robert Zoellick (2008–2012), former Trade Representative, former Deputy Secretary of State and former President of the World Bank Group

Presidents

- Bill Clinton (1991), President 1993–2001
- Gerald Ford (1964, 1966), President 1974–1977

Senators

- Tom Daschle (2008), Senator from South Dakota 1987-2005
- John Edwards (2004), Senator from North Carolina 1999–2005

�֎ Chuck Hagel (1999, 2000), Senator from Nebraska 1997–2009

�֎ John Kerry (2012), Senator from Massachusetts 1985–2012, current United States Secretary of State

✶ Sam Nunn (1996, 1997), Senator from Georgia 1972–1997

Governors

✶ Mitchell Daniels (2012) Governor of Indiana2004–present

✶ Jon Huntsman, Jr. (2012), Governor of Utah2005–2009

✶ Rick Perry (2007), Governor of Texas2000–present

✶ Mark Sanford (2008), Governor of South Carolina2003–2011

✶ Kathleen Sebelius (2008), Governor of Kansas2003-2009

Military

✶ Lyman Lemnitzer (1963), Supreme Allied Commander NATO 1963–1969

✶ Alexander Haig (1978), NATO Commander 1974–1979 (US Secretary of State1981–1982)

✶ Keith B. Alexander (2012), Commander US Cyber Command; Director, National Security Agency.

Bankers

❊ David Rockefeller, Sr. (2008, 2009, 2011), Former Chairman, Chase Manhattan Bank

❊ William Joseph McDonough (1997), former President, Federal Reserve Bank of New York

❊ Ben Bernanke (2008,[110]2009), Chairman of the Board of Governors of the United States Federal Reserve. Current Chairman of the Federal Reserve.

❊ Paul Volcker (1982, 1983, 1986, 1987, 1988, 1992, 1997, 2009, 2010), former Chairman of the Federal Reserve

Media

❊ William F. Buckley, Jr. (1996), columnist and founder of National Review

❊ George Stephanopoulos (1996, 1997), Former Communications Director of the Clinton Administration (1993–1996), now ABC NewsChief Washington Correspondent.

❊ Fouad Ajami (2012), Senior Fellow, The Hoover Institution, Stanford University

Of course this doesn't include all the players, just some of the Americans that have attended these highly secretive get-togethers. What it boils down to, is that there are approximately two hundred fifty people on our planet that control the wealth and the lives of the rest of us. That's two hundred fifty people usurping the wealth, liberty and freedom of seven billion people around the planet and in our country they are using many of the officials we elect to do so.

As I go over the next set of numbers, keep in mind that the bankers that own the Federal Reserve in concert with several politicians both past and present, are fully responsible for enslaving you and your families along with future generations to this debt.

As of this moment on this day as I write (January 28, 2013 4:30 pm CST) the National debt and the amount that you are responsible for looks like this;

Cited from the "National Debt Calculator" www.usdebt-clock.org [http://www.usdebtclock.org]

- US National Debt $16,485,446,559,671.00
- Debt per citizen (this includes your babies) $52,295.00
- Debt per taxpayer $145,961.00
- Interest owed on the debt $3,408,546,539,232.00
- Interest owed per citizen (this includes your babies) $10,486.00
- US Total Debt $58,131,340,657,455.00
- Total debt per citizen $184,406.00
- Total debt per family $732,506.00

❋ U.S. unfunded liabilities $122,475,433,978,432.00

❋ Liability per U.S. Tax payer $1,084,108.00

So, if you are a tax payer do you happen to have an extra million lying around to give the government for your share of the debt and liabilities? No you say? Guess who owns you?

Conclusion

Turning and turning in the widening gyre
The falcon cannot hear the falconer;
Things fall apart; the center cannot hold;
Mere anarchy is loosed upon the world,
The blood-dimmed tide is loosed, and everywhere
The ceremony of innocence is drowned;
The best lack all conviction, while the worst
Are full of passionate intensity.
William Butler Yeats (1865 - 1936)

Why is it important that I understand what's taking place in my world today?

To some, understanding this information will mean nothing to them. They either will choose not to believe in the facts, or it will simply be so disturbing to them that they simply will not want to deal with it. Both the government and the bankers know this and are literally banking on it. Many will continue to believe that the government that has seemed to take care of them all of their lives will continue to do so. They will continue to place their faith in the very entity that has created the situation we are in today. There are others, however, who possess as part of their character a sense of responsibility for themselves, their families and their friends. They will both take heed of this warning and search out more information to help them understand the scope of the calamity that is lurking around the very next corner in our economy.

If you can understand what is written here, you will also understand that there is a tremendous opportunity for you to prepare and have some control over both your near and long term future. There are some common sense things that you can start doing today to protect both yourself and your loved ones from the chaos that is sure to take place as the economy comes to a screeching halt. There are both measures you can take to secure your future and there are things you can do to assist your fellow Americans in releasing the death grip that the current mammoth government has on the throat of our nation.

It is imperative that we reach out to as many fellow Americans as possible and help them understand the importance of both *freedom* and our *constitution*. The constitution written by our forefathers is a document forged by men who lived under tyrannical governments. The intent of this document was to prevent exactly what is happening today in America. As dismal as things may seem, we are still protected by the constitution but only to the extent that we are willing to defend it, protect it and keep it secure for both ourselves and our future generations. The answer to what our forefathers and the citizens of this nation faced back in 1787, was individual freedom. *Individual freedom* is the answer to all of the problems our nation faces today. Individual-personal-freedom and the willingness to protect it can once again remove from our backs a government that has grown out of control and stripped these freedoms away.

This is not an impossible task, but it will take people that are willing to break the mold that party lines have created in this country. It is pure madness that is taking place today. We have bills being passed at an alarming rate that our elected officials do not even read before a vote. Both the Republican and Democratic parties are like factions that could care less about how the countless laws they either pass or oppose will affect the country. They are like little minions that cast their vote along party lines because that has simply become the norm. This behavior has spilled over into our population as well. People of these two opposing parties spew hatred towards each other. They think that they are at war over their differing philosophies when in actuality they are really one in the same. It is simply that their methods to destroy the nation are different. We have become a nation of name callers and haters, but worse of all, we have become a nation that has lost its ability to stop and think. No enemy abroad poses a greater threat to our nation than we as Americans pose to it ourselves.

Debate can and should be a healthy thing for our nation, but debate without facts or debate for the purpose of simply putting on a show is nothing short of a detriment to our society. Debate when approached with an open mind to discover a solution based on factual history or math can be, and at one time was a driving force for progress. Today however, debate has become nothing more than a willingness or need to impose one's own philosophy on another without so much as giving an ear to the opposing point of view. History and hard facts no longer have a bearing on the outcome or decisions made in the halls of the governing body of this nation, that at one time in our history served as a shining example for the rest of the world to witness. Today much of the world is laughing. It is as if *chaos* has reached a finger down into this once great melting pot and is stirring it with vigor.

We must learn quickly how to communicate with each other if we are to have any hope of saving this nation. We must learn to both communicate and *listen* with the intent of finding solutions based on fact vs. emotion. As an example, let's take a moment and speak to a current hot topic taking place in America today: Gun control and the second amendment.

Without a doubt this is a very heated topic, one that is a shining example of the chaos running rampant in our nation amongst ourselves. Personally, I am not a gun owner although I believe in the right to bear arms. The contention as I see it amongst both our politicians and much of the population is there are those who believe it is a breach of our second amendment rights to dictate to us what weapons we can have. On the other side, people argue that there would be less violence and that people should not have semi-automatic military style weapons. They believe that these types of weapons are not necessary or protected under the second amendment. Two arguments, two different point of views and if approached logically removing party lines and focusing on history and facts without all the name calling, you would think that sensible men and woman should and could, have a meaningful conversation and come to a logical conclusion. Oh no, enter *chaos* creating mud-slinging and name calling. Like silly little children, when they don't get their way will simply increase their hatred for one another and continue to use the people that they were elected to represent, as a hammer to try to force their ideals upon one another.

Yet both history and math does hold the true answer to this madness. One of our very own institutions of higher learning, in fact the highest rated learning institution not just here in our country but in the entire world did an extensive study on violence and the correlation of guns to violence. This study included not just our country, but many other modernized countries as well. The institution that I speak of is Harvard. The study, which appeared in Volume 30, Number 2 of the *Harvard Journal of Law & Public Policy* (pp. 649-694) supports via *mathematical analysis* based on *history*, that nations that have strict gun laws have a higher rate of both murders and violence than our country that has the right to bear arms. The study proved that Russia for example, who has the strictest of gun laws forbidding their citizens by and large to own them, has 4 times the violent crime rate than we do. It further supported once again via *math* and *history* that country's like Norway that has the highest rate of gun ownership also has the least amount of violent crimes. Yet in our growing chaos we refuse to listen to reason and continue to govern by emotion. It is our willingness to ignore facts, to continue to ignore history and the laws of math that continues to perpetuate the downfall of our society.

The crisis that brought gun control to the forefront of the political arena was a sad and tragic event. I cannot begin to conceive, having children myself, the pain and anguish felt by the parents of Sandy Hook Elementary. Yet, I have pondered this event and I have attempted to place myself in those parents' shoes to try and envision how I would both feel and react to this terrible event. While it is difficult for anyone who has not walked in those shoes to fully understand, I believe as a parent who loves his children dearly and as an American who loves his country and values freedom that even a greater tragedy has unfolded from this crisis. That tragedy is when a number of our politicians who possess the personal attribute's mentioned earlier in this book, will use the death of anyone of our children for their own personal gain to further control our nation.

We have allowed a variety of crises to govern us. We react without stopping to think. We have become a society in which we allow isolated occurrences to change the way an entire society is governed and lives. The nation that our forefathers left us to embrace freedom and create wealth has become a nation that embraces the false security of government, where the only things created on any grand scale are more government and literally millions of laws to govern us.

A Real Education vs. a Government Controlled Education

One of my children still in high school, started to talk to me about the Great Depression. Evidently they are reviewing this period in an AP European class. A couple of things brought up in our conversation, prompted me to ask to see the text book they are studying. I often wonder why the vast majority of our population today has such great difficulty with history. Every now and then it takes reviewing a history book like this one to remind myself once again what I discovered during my own studies many years ago to be true. This text book is so pro-socialist twisting history and advocating socialism that it is no wonder the population thinks and believes the way that they do today. This is the problem with having a government agency controlling education (*The Department of Education*) and regulating what our children will learn. This history book is so-one-sided advocating the socialist philosophy. It is written in a manner that will lead any reader to believe that government intervention is what saved the world from the Great Depression. it is so slanted without any opposing view that it is truly Orwellian. Nothing about the economist and the politicians of that time period that had an entirely different opinion (and there were many), who thought that what Roosevelt was doing then with his "New Deal" would ultimately make us a debtor nation with a society growing more government dependent.

I really don't know why this continues to surprises me. Maybe because I grew up in an era in which my generation would never imagine any form of government control over education. However, this was occurring even back in the 1980s when I was studying economics. The colleges then, just like today, only promoted literature that touted Keynesian economics and praised this philosophy for saving the nation from the depths of the Great Depression. There was no mention of how the bankers created that mess, just like the mess we are in today. I was fortunate enough to get my hands on older material, both history books and encyclopedias written prior to the World Book and Britannica versions which by-and-large omitted much of our economic history in favor of the world banks.

As a parent I am now faced with the task of presenting the other side of history to my children. The side they will never get from our educators either in high school or college. At the same time, I am faced with the realization that I probably need to wait until after the exam so the class can be passed, because to present an opposing view right now will probably mean certain failure if answering questions on the exam is done with an informed mind.

Its not that I have a problem with history books that explain *Keynesian* economics and express the views of those that supported it either then or now. What I have a problem with is ignoring either the opposing viewpoints or omitting much of history that might support a different view. This is were our education system fails under government control and it is much of the reason that chaos is so prevalent in our society today. To me, the biggest threat to the American way of life is education. It isn't that we don't have enough schools, institutions of higher learning or enough teachers. It is what we don't teach that is the threat.

Recently I have reviewed several papers from different economist addressing today's unemployment rate. The way many economist analyze this data is a true testament to an education system gone awry. Some will use the Great Depression as a baseline. They point to that period to compare either how well or how poor the country is doing when bumped up against that time line. While unemployment statistics were not kept consistently prior to the 1930s, most economists will agree that throughout the *Great Depression* the unemployment rate was in the twenty-nine percent range at its peak. There are some that will say it got as high as thirty-three percent but twenty-nine percent seems to be the most popular number. You will get no argument out of me with either of those widely accepted number.

A number of economists when comparing today's unemployment rate will make the assumption that things aren't as bad today as they were during the Great Depression. They make the claim that our unemployment rate at a rounded eight percent is less than a third of what it was during the Great Depression. Some will assert that unless and until unemployment rates start to approach the levels of the Great Depression, that we shouldn't be overly concerned about another collapse of that scale in the American economy. A common thread that I find in these writings and analysis is the lack of accountability when it comes to both history and math in their numbers.

If we examine the history for that time period and compare it to today, there are some very stark and easy to understand differences that must be taken into account in order to deliver a true mathematical analysis. As I stated earlier, unemployment numbers prior to the 1930s were relatively vague and the reason for that is documented in the history of the times. Unemployment back then was primarily calculated by the numbers of men, woman and children, people of all ages and backgrounds that were participating or standing in the *soup lines*. Counts were taken and those counts were bumped up against the population of the city, township or rural area, and when compiled together across the country, these numbers gave the government and economists of that era a general feel for the overall unemployment rate.

Prior to the Great Depression, there wasn't a welfare program, social security program or unemployment benefits. These programs were all a result of the Great Depression. This is a *very* important bit of history to understand when comparing unemployment between the 1930s and today. If we were to attempt the same methodology of unemployment calculation that gave them the twenty-nine percent rate during the Great Depression, than we would have to take all the people on welfare, social security, those drawing unemployment, along with all those that simply aren't working and possibly living on the streets and group them into a "soup line number".

Today, our government calculates unemployment by taking the number of people actually drawing unemployment benefits against the population of what they consider the *available work force*. There is no consideration given to those on welfare, social security, those whose unemployment benefits have stopped or those that are simply living on the streets in our cities. So lets examine what the numbers would look like if we used a similar methodology of calculating unemployment as what took place in the 1930s. Of course we would have to assume that if we didn't have welfare, social security or unemployment, that the only way for the recipients of these benefits to survive today would be standing in *a soup line.*

According to the US Census Bureau as of this writing, our current population is three hundred eleven million, eight hundred thousand. According to the Social Security Administration there are sixty two million, one hundred seventy five thousand total Social Security recipients. According to the US Census Survey of Income and program participation study, in the second quarter of 2011 there were one hundred eight million people on some form of Federal welfare excluding Social Security and Medicaid. Now let's do some simple math.

* Social Security Recipients 62,175,000 / Current population 311,800,000 = 20%

* Welfare Recipients 108,000,000 / 311,800,000 = 34.6%.

* United States Reported unemployment (People actually receiving unemployment benefits). = 7.7% "of the labor force"

Our 2012 total combined Soup line calculation = 62.3%

Now, can we really take the total number of Social Security recipients and the total number of Welfare recipients and throw them into our *soup line* numbers? Would it be correct to assume that they would *all* be standing in a soup line if they didn't have that particular benefit? The answer is *no*, the numbers would still be skewed. There are a number of Social Security recipients that if they lost their benefits, are either wealthy enough or still have another form of retirement income that would sustain them, keeping them out of our *soup line*. Similarly, there are a number of welfare recipients drawing benefits that supplements a poverty level income and a portion of those would probably avoid our soup line as well. So let's for grins go overboard and reduce some numbers the other way and see what it looks like. Let's just say that we generously exclude half of the welfare recipients and half of the social security recipients from our numbers to err on the side of caution.

The unemployment number using a fifty percent exclusion rate would still be thirty-five percent based on a similar methodology to calculate the unemployment numbers to that of the Great Depression. That number itself, is six percent higher than the twenty-nine percent unemployment rate recorded for that time.

What is ironic about all of this is that the programs that were initiated by the progressive Franklin Delano Roosevelt, and touted to prevent and reduce the level of poverty in our nation have proved to do just the opposite. They have not only increased poverty, but they have hidden from the population quite neatly their impacts to the economy. Unfortunately the crisis that will bring this realization to light for the citizens, will be well beyond the time they would have needed to prepare for it, and the reason for that is education. Our government controlled education.

The most educated people I know are those that have been smart enough to study well beyond their formal years of education. I believe that when it comes to history, government, economics and social science, that obtaining an education by listening to lectures from many of our current educators and studying only the required literature specified by these institutions, that much of history is missed. Winston Churchill once said that "History is written by the victors", and while he wasn't the first to either say or acknowledge this, I have found these words to be very true.

Home schooling while still an option in this country might allow for a more rounded education when it comes to delivering differing viewpoints as well as an expanded scope of what has transpired in our history or with our government. However, even the home school student is regulated by the government as to what is required to learn and agree upon to pass the required exams. While home schooling is still legal in the United States, I don't imagine that it will be very much longer before our government if left unchecked will move to ban it by law. There are a good number of socialist countries that have already made such moves. Germany, Greece, Cyprus, Albania and Sweden are just a few of the European socialist nations that have a ban on home schooling. Cuba, El Salvador, Guatemala, Greenland, Trinidad and Tobago are North American nations that have banned home schooling with Canada and the United States allowing it under strict regulations. Countries like Brazil have made home schooling illegal in South America.

Education is treated like a commodity that governments over the years have felt a need to control. An educated population can be very risky to a government whose best interest is self-serving. There is no better form of governing than Democracy when the citizens of those nations are informed. To steal the wealth of a nation that at one time knew and embraced freedom takes a level of intervention into the education system. The Department of Education regulates our schools and the outcome of this intervention is apparent amongst our population.

We MUST take our education system back from our government. The Department of Education in this country in my opinion is every bit as detrimental to the freedom of our nation as the Federal Reserve System. If we are going to allow our government to continue to control our education system, then at what point should we expect our government to force *re-education* for those of us who either don't agree or know better?

What Can We Do? What is The Fix?

"We have given the People of this Republic the greatest blessing they have ever had, their own currency to pay their own debts"
—President Abraham Lincoln 1867 (speaking about a currency owned by the people and not a group of privately owned banks like the Federal Reserve.)

"The high office of the President has been used to formant a plot to destroy the American's freedom and before I leave office I must inform the Citizen of his plight."
—President John F. Kennedy (In a speech made at Columbia University on November 12th, 1963, 10 days before he was murdered)

We have had two Presidents who put patriotism and love of their country in front of the interest of the world bankers. Both received bullets to the head for their patriotism. One was successful and paid for it with his life, while the other was assassinated in his pursuit to correct what Woodrow Wilson did to our nation. Since then, the realization of what happens when you stand up to the World Bankers has created what I consider to be a level of cowardice in the office of the Presidency as well as the halls of congress.

We must put an **end to Inflation** as well as the **Federal Reserve** and forever ban the government from ever inflating or turning over the power to control the nations money supply to private bankers ever again.

Inflation is the one single ingredient that is the ultimate game changer and the one thing that when implemented into an economy catapults a nation into socialism or when stopped can allow a nation to return to free markets and a free people. Inflation creates poverty at every level, and if eliminated under a capitalistic economic philosophy, will reduce poverty and increase wealth over the long haul. Inflation is a cancer that cannot be cured, it must be cut out!

As stated before, we are faced with the cold hard facts that our nation is now governed by those who would continue to expand the poverty levels and by doing so expand the nonproductive voting base. As long as this continues to occur, the chances of voting in politicians that have the backbone and fortitude to do what is right for the nation continues to diminish. However, if we can stop inflation all of that will change instantly. Inflation truly is the root of all the evil that has befallen this nation. It was the one ingredient that was necessary to both convert our society to socialism and to advance the progressive socialist agenda. *Inflation successfully hides for a time the ill effects of socialism.* If it wasn't for inflation, the United States today would not be a debtor nation. We would not have the level of poverty, the unsustainable entitlements, the number of burdensome regulations and there would be no discussion of a "fiscal cliff "or going over one. If the United States of America had been left uninfected by the disease of inflation, we would be much more advanced as a nation. Our society would be better educated, possess more wealth and have a much lower level of poverty. Inflation has hidden from the American public the true tax rate imposed on them, preventing our citizens their right to the information necessary in order to make educated decisions on who should govern them.

I can only tell you what I think the fix is and it isn't pretty. As a matter of fact it is down-right painful to even think about it. But the alternative to not fixing the problem is a hundred fold worse.

First, we have to stop the deception. Personally, you have to realize that we are by any economic indicator and by the intentions of a few, a *socialist nation*. We need to talk about it, we need to explain it and we have to attempt to unplug from the *matrix*, so to speak, as many fellow Americans who still have the capacity to think and reason. Then we have to understand that we cannot sustain the path we are on and continue to march in line with what is taking place in America today. It will only result in the total collapse of our nation, leaving absolutely nothing other than slavery to the government for ourselves and our future generations. We also have to understand, that the only way to effect change is by either our vote or by the sword. I totally prefer the vote method, however we are faced with an incredibly dire situation. We now have more voters dependent on the government which means without massive education and reasoning the government is protected by the votes that they feed. So where does this leave us? Many people that are able to see things for what they are, believe we have three options at this point; one is education, the other is communism and the third is revolution. Just so you know, the government is well aware that these are our only options as well. They will continue to spend at a rate to expand the dependent base and secure votes from the hungry and are in the process of promoting legislation to disarm the population using any event they can to justify this end.

If education is your preferred method, than educate yourself and educate others every single opportunity you get. Time is truly running out. I can't predict how long the government can keep things going, but I can tell you with all certainty that they are running out of the ability quickly. There are a number of nations today that are opting out of using the US dollar as the *reserve currency*. Countries like China, Iran, Pakistan and India are either moving to hard money (gold), to trade with each other or are in the process of solidifying agreements to use their own currencies. As this trend continues, the result here at home will be huge price swings in our economy as the dollars floating outside of our country come home to roost. Once again, turn on your T.V. and use it for a little more than entertainment. Understanding what inflation has done to the dollar and tracking its downfall over the last one hundred years, I don't believe that the dollar will maintain its *reserve status* beyond 2014, if we do not immediately stop inflating it. I believe that the numbers point to hyperinflation as the dollar loses its reserve status and that when this event occurs the American standard of living will be reduced overnight by twenty-five percent. When this comes to pass, Americans will experience what every citizen of every other nation has experienced when their government has hyperinflated their currency. Prices will double every twenty-four hours for an extended period of time while the government scrambles to create another fiat currency they can force us to use. The social chaos that will ensue will be beyond the comprehension of most ill prepared Americans and most of these

Americans will call for their government to become exactly what we were-never-ever meant to be. Instead of America continuing on throughout history, America as we know it will simply become history, just another lesson amongst many, of what *inflation* does to a nation.

A radical change must be made in our country if you want to have anything left for your children or our nation's future generations. From an economic stand point, the only way we can turn back *socialism* and return this country to *capitalism* the way it was intended, is to suffer both a depression and then swiftly return to our founding principles laid out by our Forefathers. Knowing that we are going to have a depression doesn't make me a prophet. Outside of biblical writings, I've never known there to be any prophets. People that are able to glimpse the future do it by understanding real historical facts, see the present for what it is ,and have an understanding of the only true science known to man, *math*.

If I were to take a pot of water, put it on the stove, place a finger in the water and turn the heat up under the pot, understanding and knowing what is going to eventually happen does not make me a prophet. I can by having an understanding of both history and math with a one hundred percent confidence level and accuracy predict several things. I can predict at what temperature I will need to remove my finger so that it will not get burnt. I can predict how long I would need to leave my finger in the water as it heated up and at what temperature it would take to cause irreparable damage to my finger. I can even predict how long I could leave my finger in the water as the temperature increased to the point in which it starts to burn me, but if I remove it at a specific time and temperature, even though I may feel pain for several days or even weeks, with the correct treatment the pain will go away and my finger will be as good as new. Today, we are at a point with inflation that if we don't remove it from the pot so-to-speak, it will cause irreversible damage and we will lose our nation. However if we stop it, completely remove it, we will have to deal with some pain, but our nation will heal and it could come bouncing back with a vengeance.

There will be those who will tell you that inflation is ok in a modern growing world and necessary to prevent starvation and poverty. For those who believe that I simply say, "Look at the world today." The lie to that thought process is right in front of you in the inflated debt of nations and the expanded poverty it is causing. There will be others that will tell you that if we stop inflation now that it will be the end of society and possibly the world. That people will suffer greatly and we will never recover. This is exactly the lie that the bankers and some members of our government will have you believe so that they can continue to amass huge personal fortunes and secure unimaginable power over not just us but every nation on the planet. No doubt, there will be some suffering, but if enough people are aware of what has taken place we can swiftly move beyond any momentary suffering and come back with a very secure and strong future for America, becoming once again that shining star on the hill for all of mankind.

I know the depression part is very unpalatable and hard to accept, but it's a mathematical inevitability. Without a doubt, we are going to have a depression. A depression is a method of correction when things are going wrong in an economy. They are a fact of life and absolutely as inevitable as having a hurricane, a tornado, or an earthquake. Unfortunately, when a government intervenes in an economy, depressions become national and depending on the type of depression they can and will change an entire nations economic and or political philosophy.

As I see it, the real choices are, what type of depression we are willing to allow. As discussed earlier, there are two types of Depressions; deflationary depression or hyper-inflationary depression and I promise you, one is severely worse than the other.

If you understand what I have written and you believe this to be true, then you may want to take the following actions:

❋ Start to obtain a food storage: There are many companies out there were you can purchase anywhere from a 3 months to several years supply depending on your means. Understand this one very important fact: You do not want to become a liability for someone else to take care of. There will be an overwhelming number of people left in that position.

❋ If you have the means, start saving silver and or gold. This is historically the only form of real money and whether we deflate or hyper-inflate real money will be increasingly valuable. The U.S. dollar is not real money. It is a currency backed by little more than a false theory. If you can afford to do this great, but if you have to make a choice between storing food or real money, choose food. It will become the most valuable asset you could have. You can't eat money.

* Arm yourself. I suggest both a handgun and a rifle. Teach your children gun safety and make sure they know how to use these weapons.

* Reduce your debt so that your bills are at a minimum.

* If you are renting, now may be a good time to purchase a home vs. renting one. The Homestead Act may protect you from confiscation during a depression, but that is a big maybe!

* Get acquainted with like-minded people. You will need friends that position themselves like you do and are not looking to take what you have. Hunger is a very strong motivator. Ponder that thought for a bit and imagine what you might do if you had no food and water. What would you do to get those things for you and your family? I recommend that you purchase the book, "A Failure of Civility", this book could save both you and your loved ones life in the coming crisis.

* Educate, educate, and educate as many people that will listen to you. Educate yourself and educate others, this is truly our only hope for the future. Take it seriously and do it religiously. Do not let others discourage you and expect that most people will not want to hear what you have to say. Understand that those dependent on the government, either working for it or financially dependent on it, will battle you

every step of the way in order to continue to secure their own personal well-being.

❋ Put our country first before your own personal needs. Don't mistake what I say here for putting our government first. There is a huge difference. We must support members of our government that support individual freedom and defend the constitution. It is our duty as Americans to not support members of our government that do not abide by their oath to do the same.

❋ Vote only for those running for Political offices that are like minded, freedom loving, constitutional supporting Americans. This shouldn't be too hard to do because currently there are only a few. Look to the Libertarian party and possibly a handful of the younger politicians in the republican party for political candidates that tend to be of the same mind set. Politicians like Ron Paul should be an example and indeed a litmus test that we judge all other politicians by. The old guard in the Republican party is every bit as tainted as the majority of the Democratic party. In my opinion voting for any candidate that does not have at the top of their platform ending the FED and inflation simply isn't worth a vote. Keep this in mind even as you look at the younger republicans.

❋ Get involved if you can in politics, host events in your home, talk at churches or other forums, forward information like this to your friends and family and prompt everyone you can to action.

❋ Most importantly, do not back down from what you believe in. The truth is a strong weapon as long as we stand for the truth and don't turn our backs on it. The real challenge in our society today is talking to each other about the truth and what is real vs. arguing, fighting, kicking and screaming about it like two-year-old's.

I know many people who have studied economics that have put out snippets of information educating people about what has and is taking place in both America and around the globe. More often than not, they inform just enough to scare people into buying some form of investment consulting advisory letter under the guise that they will lead them to financial freedom if they pay for their advice. While many are absolutely correct in the snippets of information they use to entice, you simply do not need an investment consultant. If you are smart enough to understand what is written here, you already know what you should start doing to protect yourself, especially if you are the average American who is barely making ends meet. Those things I have already laid out for you above.

My goal is to educate as many people as I can and to get others to educate as many as they can. I do this for both my children and yours and hopefully to save our country for future generations to come. There isn't much time left and there is much to do. This is not an impossible task.

Education at this point is not going to prevent the coming depression, but education will allow us to both shorten a depression and return our country to the free, strong nation that we were before we allowed the world bankers to get their hands on it. This is our time in history. Others before us have laid down their lives and shed their blood so that we could enjoy the freedoms and liberties of a once great nation. Will we be willing to make the necessary sacrifices to restore our nation to that of what those before us shed their blood to give us? Or will we go down in history as a nation of self-indulgent people, unwilling to stand up for our freedom and sovereignty in favor of economic slavery for our future generations?

We must not allow the government the ability to take away our guns. This includes the current ban they are trying to impose on assault weapons. Assault weapons may be needed one day to defend the constitution and throw tyranny from our backs, as is our right and duty as Americans. Guns are absolutely necessary in the citizens hands to defend against a government that would enslave them. If we allow the government any infringement on our 2nd Amendment rights we will not survive. Write your congressmen and senators. Keep up the pressure so they know that if they attempt to circumvent the constitution it will be at their political peril. I simply cannot stress this enough.

Understand that there are members of our government that have and will continue to use any crisis it can come up with to persuade the people into giving up more and more of their rights. They will spin, lie, deceive and use whatever means to accomplish their goals for the elite simply because they think they will be protected when the house of cards comes tumbling down.

Start your own grassroots organizations. Talk at churches, social groups or anywhere that people will listen. Above all keep in mind that people do not want to wake up. Their dream state is like a security blanket and for many that blanket will have to burn from around them before they will come to. Help who you can and move on from those that simply refuse to learn.

While most people in my position will ignore the poor dependent part of our nation, both writing them off as a lost cause and considering them just people that will always vote for those in government that will feed them, I am of a differing opinion. It is those people we need to reach out to the most. Just because someone is poor and receiving welfare doesn't mean that they don't have a brain. These are the people that will get sacrificed up and annihilated first once the coming Great Depression occurs. They are the ones who really do not know or understand that while the government has used them to both gain and stay in office, that they will be the first ones sent to slaughter as the economy falls apart.

The poor by and large live in densely populated cities and when the depression hits they will have absolutely nothing. Their neighborhoods, districts and cities will implode. Hunger and panic will drive them into the streets in search of food for themselves and their children and they will kill each other to get whatever they can to survive. The poor simply have no idea how the government and bankers have used them. They have no idea that they are poor by intent and that the government they supported because they felt it was their only means of survival will be the government who points their military machines at them first. There will be absolutely nothing they can do about it. Those that are ignorant in the middle and upper class will condone it simply because they are afraid of the poor making it out of these cities in attempts to come for the little they have left to survive.

While it is the poor that the government depended on for their survival, it is the poor that we must focus on to reverse that trend. While there are those that simply prefer to let the government take care of them, we must realize that it is the government that intentionally created their environment so that they could use them. There are many poor people just like any other people who would love a better life but for the life of them, cannot understand how they can throw off the poverty that binds them. I believe that once poor people start to understand, that their lives have been enslaved by a government. A government whose intent was to keep them there and that soon they will be like cattle slaughtered up as if they created the nation's problems, that they could raise up like a title wave and be the driving force needed to return this nation to freedom.

Oddly enough, the people many like to blame for our nations problems are the very people that we must reach and educate for our very survival as a nation. Always remember, the government would not have been able to become the overpowering government they are today, if they hadn't created the dependency necessary to steal the wealth of our nation. Poor people are not the problem, it's the government that made them poor and keeps them poor that is the problem. We simply cannot ignore the poor and we must do everything we can to prepare them to survive the coming depression and do it without the government. We must do everything as human beings to educate and this will take patience, understanding and commitment. To fail will surely mean the downfall of the nation altogether.

While I will not sell you financial advice, I feel that it is imperative as I hope you do, that we get this message into the hands of every single American we can, and that does cost money. If you feel like you have the means to help us get the word out, you can go to *www.freedomslost.net* [http://www.freedomslost.net/], and make a donation. Your financial contribution will allow us the funds to advertise, print more copies of this book and distribute this information to other Americans like yourself. You can also encourage your friends and relatives to get copies of this book. I am in this to help save our nation, not to profit from its current state.

A Message to the Thieves of Nations

I have been a thief so I know a thief. I have been a swindler so I know a swindler. I have been a con man so I know a con man. I have been thrown into the bowels of your worst penitentiaries at an early age and I have pulled myself up out of the depths of hell to become the man I am today. You educated me.

Today I am the average American. I am the one that you fear the most. I am able to see and understand what you have done just as many now are beginning to see. I place my country well above you and I pledge my allegiance and my life to standing steadfast in your way. While integrity, loyalty, honesty, truth and God are lost on you, it will be these very virtues that founded our nation that will haunt and destroy you. We are coming in numbers that you will never stop.

FastPencil
http://www.fastpencil.com